Georg Manville Fenn

The Bag of Diamonds

Georg Manville Fenn

The Bag of Diamonds

ISBN/EAN: 9783743320598

Manufactured in Europe, USA, Canada, Australia, Japa

Cover: Foto ©ninafisch / pixelio.de

Manufactured and distributed by brebook publishing software (www.brebook.com)

Georg Manville Fenn

The Bag of Diamonds

THE BAG OF DIAMONDS.

BY

GEORGE MANVILLE FENN,

Author of "The Master of the Ceremonies," "Double Cunning," Etc.

THE
ARTHUR WESTBROOK COMPANY
Cleveland, Ohio, U. S. A.

Printed in the United States of America

THE BAG OF DIAMONDS.

CHAPTER I.

IN A FOG.

"Ugh! what a night! And I used to grumble about Hogley Marsh! Why, it's like living in a drain!"

Ramillies Street, W. C., was certainly not attractive at twelve o'clock on that December night, for it had been snowing in the early part of the evening; that snow was suffering from a fall of blacks; and as evil communications corrupt good manners, the evil communication of the London soot was corrupting the good manners of the heavenly snow, which has become smirched by the town's embrace, and was sorrowfully weeping itself away in tears beneath a sky—

No, there was not any sky. For four days there had not been a breath of air to dissipate the heavy mist, and into this mist the smoke of a million chimneys had rolled, mingled, and settled down in the streets in one horrible yellowish-black mirk.

There were gas lamps in Ramillies Street—here and there distinguishing themselves by a faint glow overhead; but John Whyley, policeman on the beat, was hardly aware of their existence till he laid his hand upon each post.

"Now, only that Burglar Bill & Co. aren't such fools as to come out on such a night as this, here's their chance. Why, they might burgle every house on one side of the street while the whole division was on the other. Blest if I know hardly where I am!"

J. W. stopped and listened, but it seemed as if utter silence as well as utter darkness had descended upon the great city. But few people were about, and where a vehicle passed along a neighboring street the patter of hoofs and roll of wheels was hushed by the thick snow.

"It is a puzzler," muttered the man. "Blind man's buff's nothing to it, and no pretty gals to catch. Now, whereabouts am I? I should say I'm just close to the corner by the square, and—well, now, look at that!"

He uttered a low chuckle, and stared up from the curbstone at a dull, red glare that seemed like the eye of some fierce monster swimming in the sea of fog, and watching the man upon his beat.

"And if I didn't think I was t'other side of the street! Ah, how you do 'member me of old times," he continued, apostrophizing the red glare; "seems like being back at Hogley, and looking off the station platform to see if you was burning all right after I'd been and lit you up. Red signals for trains—red signals for them as wants help," he muttered as, with his hands within his belt, he stepped slowly up under an arch of iron scroll-work rusting away, a piece of well-forged ornamentation, which had once borne an oil lamp, and at whose sides were iron extinguishers, into which, in the bygone days when Ramillies was a fashionable street, footmen had thrust their smoking links. But fashion had gone afar, and Ichabod was written metaphorically upon the door of that old Queen Anne house, while really there was a tarnished brass plate bearing the inscription "Dr. Chartley," with blistered panels above and below. Arched over the doorstep was an architect's idea of a gigantic shell, supported by two stout boys, whom a lively imagination might have thought to be suffering from the doctor's prescriptions, as they glared wildly at the red bull's eye in the centre of the fanlight above the door.

"Nothing like a red signal to show you where you are," said John Whyley, stepping slowly back on to the pavement, to the very edge of the curbstone, and then keeping to it as his guide for a few yards, till he had passed a second door, also displaying the red light, and beneath it, in letters nearly rubbed away, though certainly not from cleaning, the word "Surgery."

"That's where that young nipper of a buttons lives, him as took a sight at me when I ketched him standing on his head a-top of the dustbin down the area. Hullo!"

John Whyley stood perfectly still and invisible in the fog, as the surgery door was opened; there was a low scuffling noise, and a hurried whispering.

"Get your arm well under him. Hold hard! Shut the door. Mind he don't slip down. It's dark as pitch. Now then, come on."

At that moment a bright light shone upon the scene in front of Dr. Chartley's surgery door, for John Whyley gave a turn to the top of the bull's-eye lantern looped on to his belt, and threw up the figures of three men, two of whom were supporting on either side another, whose head hung forward and sidewise, whose legs were bent, and his body in a limp, helpless state, which called forth all the strength of the others to keep him from subsiding in a heap upon the snow. He seemed to be young, heavily bearded, and, as far as his costume could be seen in the yellow glare, he wore high boots and a pea-jacket; while his companions, one of whom was a keen-faced man, with clean-shaved face and a dark moustache, the other rather French-looking from his shortly cropped beard, wore ulsters and close traveling-caps.

As the light flashed upon the group, one of the men drew his breath sharply between his teeth, and for a space no one stirred.

"Acciden', gentlemen?" said John Whyley, giving a sniff as if he smelt a warm sixpence, but it was only caused by the soot-charged fog.

The constable's speech seemed to break the spell, and one of the men spoke out thickly:

"Ax'den', constable? Yes, it's all right. Hold him up, Smith. Wants to lie down, constable. Thinks snow is clean sheets."

"Oh, that's it, is it, sir?" said John Whyley, examining each face in turn a little suspiciously. "Thought as it was a patient—"

"Yes," said the man with the moustache, speaking in a high-pitched voice, "doctor keeps some good stuff. Not all physic, policeman. Here, hold up." This last to the man he was supporting, and upon whose head he now placed a soft felt hat, which he had held in his hand.

"Gent seems rather on, sir," said John Whyley, going up more closely.

"Ah!" said the first speaker, "you smelt his breath."

"'Nough to knock you down, sir," said the constable. "He'll want to come and see the doctor again to-morrow morning."

There was a very strong odor of spirits, and in the

gloom it did not occur to the constable that the two men who seemed most intoxicated were very bright-eyed, and yet ghastly p¹e. He merely drew back for the group to pass.

"Got to take him far, sir?"

"Far? No, constable. Let him lie down and go to sleep. Dishgusting thing man can't come to see friend without getting drunk. Look at me—and Shmith."

"Yes, sir; you're all right enough," said the constable. "Shall I lend you a hand?"

"No," said the man with the moustache, "we're all right; get us a cab."

"Where, sir,?" said the constable, with a grin; don't believe such a thing's to be got, sir, a night like this. All gone home."

At that moment from out of the fog there was a sudden jolt and the whish of a whip.

"Hullo?" shouted the policeman.

"Hullo!" came back in a husky voice, as if spoken through layers of flannel, "what street's this?"

"Ramillies. Here's a fare."

There was a muttering, then a bump, jolt, and jangle of a cab heard, and a huge figure slowly seemed to loom up out of the fog in a spectral way, leading a gigantic horse, beyond which was something dark.

"What's the row?" said the husky voice.

"These gents want a cab."

"Oh, but I can't drive nowheres to-night. I drove right into one pub, and then nearly down two areas. Where do you want to go."

"John's Hotel, Surrey Street, old man. Look sharp. Five bob."

"Five what, sir? Why, I wouldn't stir a step under ten. I'm just going to get my old horse into the first mews, shove on his nosebag and then get inside and go to sleep. I can't drive. I shall have to lead him."

"Give him ten," said the man with the sharp voice.

"All right. Here, hold up, old man," said the other. "Look sharp! See if ever I come out with him again."

"Yes, don't make a noise, or you'll bring out the doctor," said the other man, and the policeman went to the cab door.

The cab evidently objected to the fare, for the door stuck, and only yielded at last with a rattle, and so suddenly that John Whyley nearly went on his back; but he recovered himself, and held his light so that the utterly helpless man, who seemed as if composed of jelly, was pulled by one of his companions, thrust by the other, into the cab, and forced up on the back seat.

"There y'are, const'ble," said the man with the thick voice, "there's something to get glass; but don't take too much—like that chap—my deares' frien', it's s'prising ain't it? Tell cabman John's Hotel."

"All right, sir, he knows. Go ahead, cabby."

He took a few slow steps towards where the cabman stood by the horse's head.

"Think they're all right?" said the cabman, in a husky wisper.

"Give me half-a-crown," said John Whyley.

"Did they? Wish I'd stood out for a sov."

As he spoke he started his horse slowly, and the cab went by the constable, whose lamp showed the interior very indistinctly, the cab window being drawn up, and then the sight and sound of the vehicle died out in the fog, and all was once more still.

"Ill wind as blows no one any good!" said the cox-stable, slowly continuing his beat. "Rather have my half-crown than their sick headaches in the morning. Rather rum that no one came out with all that talking."

John Whyley hummed a tune and tried two or three front doors and area gates, and then he took off his helmet and scratched his head as if puzzled.

"Now, have I done right?" he said suddenly. "Seemed to be square. Smelt of drink horrid. Other two 'peared to be on all but once or twice. I say! Was it acting?"

He gave his helmet a sharp blow with his doubled fist, stuck it on tightly, and took a few quick steps in the direction in which the cab had moved off."

"Tchah!" he ejaculated, stopping short; "that's the worst o' my trade; makes a man suspicious of everything and everybody. Why, I nearly accused the missus of picking my pockets of that sixpence I forgot I spent with a mate. It's all right. They were as tight as tight. Ugh! What a night."

John Whyley's beat took him in another direction, but something—a feeling of dissatisfaction with his late act, or the suspicion engendered by his calling—made him turn back and go slowly to the doctor's door.

All was perfectly still; the red lamp burned over the principal door, while over the surgery door the three last letters were more indistinct than ever, and "Surg" somehow looked like a portion of "Resurgam" on a memorial stone.

John Whyley went close up to the latter door, and listened. All was still.

He hesitated a few moments, and then tapped and listened again, when there seemed to be a slight rustling sound within, but he could not be sure.

Turning on his light, there, beside him, was a bell-pull with the hole half-filled with snow.

"Shall I?" he said, hesitating. "People don't like being called up for a cock-and-bull story, and what have I got to say? These gents came away tight."

He paused and removed his helmet for another refreshing scratch.

"Was it acting? I've heerd a chap on the stage drawl just like that one with the thick voice. Now, stop a moment. Let's argufy. Couldn't be burglary. Yes, it could—body burglary!"

John Whyley grew excited as a strange train of thought ran through his head in connection with what he had heard tell about surgeons and their investigations, and purchases delivered in the dead of night.

"I don't care," he said; "wrong or right, I wish I hadn't let that cab go, and I'll get to the bottom of it before I've done."

It might have been connected with visions of another possible half-crown, or it might have been in an honest desire to do his duty as a guardian of the public safety. At any rate, John Whyley gave a vigorous tug at Dr. Chartley's night-bell and waited.

"No answer; that's a suspicious fact," he said to himself; and he rang again, listened, waited, and rang again.

Hardly had the wire ceased to grate, when a curious whispering voice, close to his ear, said "What is it?" so strangely that John, who had only been a year in London, bounded back into the snow, and half drew his truncheon.

"What is it? Who's there?" came then.

"What a fool I am! Speaking trumpet!" muttered the man, and directing his light toward the doorpost he saw a raised patch of snow, which upon being removed displayed a hole.

To this, full of confidence now, John Whyley applied his lips.

"Police!" he said. "Anything wrong?"

There was a pause, and then the same strange voice came again.

"Wait. I'll come down."

Waiting was cold work, and John Whyley took a trot up, and was returning when he saw a dim light shine through the long glazed slits at the sides of the principal door, and directly after he heard a click as if a candlestick were set down on a marble slab, and one of the narrow windows showed a human shape in a misty way.

The bull's-eye was turned on, and, after the momentary glimpse of a face, the rattling of a chain was heard, and the front door was opened a few inches to reveal a pale, haggard, but very handsome face, with large lustrous eyes, which looked dilated and strange.

"I did not understand you, policeman. Is anything the matter?"

"Well, Miss, that's for you to say;" and he related what he had seen.

"It is very strange. My father's door is locked, and there is no light."

"Yes, Miss—one over the door."

"Yes, but that only shines into the surgery. My brother has not come back."

"But the doctor had company, Miss: that gentleman who had taken too much."

"Oh, no; impossible."

"Then I *have* been done!" cried the man, striking

his left hand a blow with his fist, as if to clinch the thought which had been troubling him.

"I don't understand you."

"Well, Miss, I'm afraid there's something wrong. But the doctor?"

"He is not in his room."

"But how about the speaking trumpet?"

"I heard the night bell. He is not in his chamber, and the passage door is locked. Perhaps—" a few moments' pause; then in a firm decided tone, "Yes you had better come in."

The door was closed, so that the chain could be unfastened; and as the door was being reopened, John Whyley pulled himself together, and cleared his throat.

"Don't be alarmed, Miss," he said, as he stood in the large blank hall, and rubbed his shoes upon a very old mat. "I don't like scaring you but its better to make sure than to let anything go wrong. That's partly, you see, Miss, what we're for."

"Yes, yes; but come at once to the surgery."

"One minute, Miss," said the constable, examining carefully the handsome frightened face, and noting that its owner was tall, graceful, rather dark, and about three or four and twenty, while though her hair was in disorder as if from lying down, the lady was fully dressed.

"What do you want?" she said, with the wild look in her eyes intensifying.

"To do everything in order, Miss. First, who lives here?"

"My father, Dr. Chartley."

"Who else on the premises?"

"The servant-girl. Our boy. My brother, a medical student, lives here, but he has not yet returned. He is at a friend's house—a little party."

"And you've had a party here, Miss?"

"Oh, no; we never have company."

"That'll do, Miss. Now for the surgery. One moment: your name, please?"

"Richmond Chartley."

"That'll do. Rum name," he muttered; and following the lady, who led the way with a chamber candlestick in past the open door of a gloomy-looking dining-room, constable John Whyley found himself at the end of a passage to the left, in front of a half-glass door, whose panes were covered on the other side by a thick dark blind.

"My father's surgery," said the lady in answer to an inquiring look.

The constable nodded, and tried the door twice before kneeling down and holding his light to the keyhole.

"Key in," he said gruffly, "locked inside. Who's likely to be here?"

"My father. He always sits in the consulting-room beyond at night—studying."

Another short nod, and the constable rapped loudly. No response.

He rapped again, with the same result. Then he drew a long breath, and the man showed that he possessed feeling as well as decision.

"I don't want to alarm you, Miss, but I ought to force open this door."

"But you do alarm me, man. Yes, you are right. No! let me come."

She rapped smartly on the door.

"Father! Father! Are you here?"

Still no reply; and she drew back, looking wildly in the constable's eyes, while her hands seemed as if drawn together to clasp each other and check the nervous trembling and be of mutual support.

"Yes," she said, "force it open. Stop! break one of the panes."

The constable leaned his shoulder against the pane nearest the lock, and there was a sharp crackling noise, the splintered glass being caught by the blind inside; but as the man thrust his hand through the great hole he had made, to draw the blind on one side, a fragment or two fell, making a musical tinkling.

The man's next act was to take his lantern from his belt, and pass it through, directing the light in all directions, as he peered through the glass above, and then he withdrew the light with a low "Ha!"

"What can you see?"

"Hold hard, please, Miss, and keep back. This isn't ladies' work. I want some help here."

"Then something has happened?"

"Well, Miss, seeing what I did see to-night, it may be nothing worse than a drop too much, but it looks ugly!"

"Who is it? My father?"

"Can't say, Miss. Elderly gent with bald head."

"Oh, what you say is possible! Quick! burst open the door!"

The constable placed his shoulder to the door, but drew back with an angry gesture.

"Of course!" he muttered, and thrusting his arm through, he reached the lock, turned the key, and the door swung open with a dismal creak.

"Now, Miss, I'll see first, and come back and tell you."

"Man! do you think I am a child?" was the sharp

reply; and rushing by him, the speaker passed into the room, and went down upon her knees directly beside a figure in a shabby old dressing-gown, lying face downward on the floor.

"Is he—"

"Quick! turn on that gas."

The constable took a step to obey, and kicked against something which rattled as it flew forward, and struck the wainscot board, while the next moment a dim, blue spark of light in a ground-glass burst into a flame, and lit up a dingy-looking, old-fashioned surgery just as the kneeling girl uttered a piteous cry.

"That's enough," muttered the constable, stooping and picking up the object he had kicked against—a short whalebone-handled life-preserver, and slipping it into his pocket. "Tells tales. Now, Miss," he continued aloud, bending over the prostrate figure. "Hah! yes! I thought as much."

It was plain enough. A slight thread of blood was trickling slowly from a spot on the smooth glistening bald head of the prostrate man, while as, with a moan of anguish, the girl thrust her arm softly beneath his neck, and raised the head, the mark of another blow was visible above the temple.

"Now, Miss, I can't leave you like this. Let me stay while you go for help. We must have some one here."

These words seemed to rouse the girl into fierce action, and she gently supported the wounded head, her hand sought the injured man's wrist, and seized it in a professional way.

"Man," she cried with angry energy, "while we are seeking help he may— Yes; still beating. Quick! Open that door. No, no; that's the way into the street! The other door—the consulting-room. Prop it open with a chair. We must get him on to the sofa, and do something at once."

"Yes, Miss; but a doctor."

"I am a doctor's daughter, man, and know what to do. Quick!"

"Well, of all—" muttered the constable, as he proceeded to the door in question; and then, without finishing the sentence, "Well, she is a plucked one!"

He stepped into a shabbily furnished room, in whose grate a fire was just aglow; and as the door swung to, and he cast the light round to seek for a chair, he caught sight of a vacant couch, a table with bottle, glasses, and sugar thereon, and the cover drawn all on one side, so that the glasses were within an ace of being off; and then, drawing in his breath, he stepped to the other side of the table, and held down the light, which fell upon a drawn and ghastly face, while, hidden by the table cover, there lay the figure of a well-dressed man.

"Fit," muttered the constable, bending lower. "No; I ain't a doctor, but I know what that means."

He stepped back quickly, and shut the door after him.

"No, no! prop it open."

"Let it be, Miss, he replied sternly. "There's something else wrong there."

The girl stared up at him aghast.

"Here's a sofy will do," he continued, pointing to a kind of settee, cushioned, and with a common moreen valance hanging down, while a rough kind of pillow was fastened to one end. "You get up, Miss, and lift a bit. I won't hurt him more than I can help. That's it. Sorry, Miss, I thought what I did."

A low moan escaped the sufferer as he was lifted

with difficulty upon the rough settee, and this being done, the constable renewed his request.

"Now, Miss, it's a thing as wants doing at once. Call help."

"Hold up his head," was the quick imperious reply; and as the man obeyed, he saw to his surprise the girl go quickly to the row of shelves at one side of the room, take down a labelled bottle, remove the stopper, and pour some of its contents into a graduated glass. To this she added a portion of the contents of another bottle, taking them down, replacing stoppers, and proceeding in the most matter-of-fact, business-like way, as if accustomed to the task, and returning to try and trickle a little fluid between the patient's lips, supplementing it by bathing his temples.

This done, she ran to a drawer, to return with a roll and scissors; then getting sponge, water, and basin, and proceeding deftly to bathe and strap up the bleeding wound, before turning to her assistant, who looked dim, as the fog seemed to have filtered into the room.

"Now," she said sharply, "is there some one injured in that room?"

"Yes, Miss; but stop. I will have help now" said the constable hoarsely. "You shan't go in there!"

At that moment, as the man stepped before the consulting-room door, there was the quick rattle of a latch-key heard faintly from the front door, and as the opening door affected that of the surgery, and made it swing slightly and creak, the girl ran to it.

"Here, Hendon! quick!"

There was a heavy step in the passage, and a young man, who looked flushed, hurried into the surgery, hat in hand, his ulster over his arm.

"What's the matter?" he said thickly. The constable directed at him a sharp glance.

"I don't know. Look! My father attacked, and —Oh! Hendon, pray, pray see!"

The young man had evidently been drinking, and the suddenness of this encounter seemed for a moment to confuse him; but as he caught sight of the injured doctor, the policeman peering at him with a sternly inquiring look, and the tall, handsome girl, with wild eyes and parted lips, pointing towards the consulting-room door, he threw back his head, gave it a shake as if to clear it, and spoke more clearly.

"Accident?" he said. "Look?"

"Yes, for pity's sake, look."

He strode to the consulting-room door, stepped in and was turning to come back, but the policeman was following.

"What is it?" he said. "Here! a light."

He snatched the lantern from the constable's hand, and the light fell directly upon the face of the prostrate figure beyond the table.

"Who's this?" he said, going down on one knee. "Why, constable, what's up? This man is dead!"

"Yes, sir, I see that."

"Yes, quite dead. But what does it mean? Has my sister—"

"Seen him? No, sir, I wouldn't let her come. Now, then, as you're here, I'll go for a doctor and some of our men."

"One minute. I'm a medical student—bit thick, constable—been at a party—but I know what I'm doing. Yes, this man's dead—shot, I think. But my father? Here, come back. That poor girl must be half wild."

He ran back into the surgery.

"Here, Rich, my girl, this is a terrible business. Yes, yes," he added, slowly examining what his sister had done, and then drawing in his breath, as he passed his hand over the smooth bald head "How did it happen?"

"I—I don't know," gasped the girl, wildly; and now that the burden was partly shifted from her shoulders, her feminine nature began to reassert itself, and she uttered a low wail.

"But—here, constable, how did this come about?"

The man explained in a few words, all the time gazing searchingly at the inquirer, but shaking his head to himself, as if feeling that the suspicions he harbored were wrong.

"And now, sir, I must have some one in," said the man in conclusion.

"Yes; of course, of course. But my father? We cannot leave him like that. To take him up to his bedroom would not be wise, and we cannot—here, Rich, I say, where are you? Constable, help me carry out this sofa."

John Whyley followed, and the comfortable couch was carried from its neighborhood by the ghastly figure lying beyond the table, into the surgery, placed close to the wall, and the wounded man carefully placed upon it in an easier position.

"Now, sir, just one look round," said the constable, as Richmond knelt down, weeping silently by her father's side, "and then I'm off. Got this, sir"

He drew out the life-preserver, and showed it to the young student before going into the consulting-room, and after a glance round, kneeling by the dead man to make a rapid search of his pockets.

"Surely this is not necessary now?"

"Yes, sir, it is. One of the first questions my sergeant will ask me will be about recognitions. That will do, sir. Not a scrap of anything about him after a sooperficial search. Now the other place."

He returned to the surgery, looked round, peered into a closet, and then examined the door.

"No signs of violence," he said; and then the settee caught his attention, and he advanced cautiously, drew up the valance, but only to reveal that it was a great chest, and had not harbor beneath for concealment of person or article connected with the case. "Chest, eh?" he said; and placing his hand to the cushion, he found that it was fastened to the great lid, which he raised with one hand, and directed the light into it with the other; but before it was open many inches he banged it down and started away as if horrified.

"Bah, man! scared by a few bones. Articulations, and preparations used in surgical lectures."

"Yes, I see," said the man, recovering himself, "but coming upon 'em sudden like, they looked rather horrid. Now, sir, I'm off. I shall send on the first of our men I see, and come back with the doctor. One two streets off, ain't there? if I can find him in the fog."

"Yes; Mr. Clayton Bell. Be quick."

The man hurried off, and in a remarkably short time, or so it seemed to the brother and sister, who were conversing in whispers as they strove to restore the unconscious man to consciousness, there was a ring at the bell, and the constable had returned with a grave, portly-looking surgeon and a sergeant of police.

"Yes," said the newcomer, after a careful examination, "two heavy blows, given, I should say, the first from behind, the second as Dr. Chartley was turning round. As you surmised, Mr. Chartley, the skull is fractured, and there is a severe pressure upon the brain. And the other case?"

The surgeon was led into the next room, where a long and careful examination was made.

"No, Mr. Chartley, no firearms here; the man has been poisoned."

"Poisoned!" cried Hendon Chartley, turning to the table, and taking up one of the glasses to raise it to his nose, and then touch the liquid in the bottom with the tip of his finger and taste it. "Brandy," he said. "only pure brandy."

He set it down, and took up the second glass, which he smelt.

"Ha! there's something here," he cried; and dipping his finger again, he tasted it, and spat quickly two or three times, before passing the glass to the surgeon, who contented himself with raising it to his nostrils.

"Yes; Mr. Chartley; no doubt about that," he said. "How did all this come about?"

He turned to the young student, who looked at the sergeant, and the sergeant at John Whyley, while the latter stared stolidly at the surgeon.

"That's what we're going to see, sir," said Whyley.

"Quite right, my man, quite right. Now, Mr. Chartley, I can do no more here. I should like to have in a colleague in consultation over your father's case. Nothing more can be done now. We will be here quite early."

He gave a few directions as he passed through the consulting-room, and then son and daughter were left to their painful vigil, and the thick fog covered all as with a funeral pall.

CHAPTER II.
GOING BACKWARDS.

BREAKFAST-TIME in the dull dining-room, with its sombre old furniture, carpet dotted with holes worn by the legs of chairs, and the drab-painted panelled walls, made cheerful by a set of engravings in tarnished gilt, fly-specked frames of the princes of the blood royal: H. R. H. the Prince Regent, with his brothers the Dukes of York, Clarence, Kent, Cumberland, Sussex, and Cambridge, each with a little square tasselled pillow at the top of the frame, and, reposing thereon, a very shabby coronet; while the two windows, with their faded curtains, looked across a row of rusty spikes at a prospect composed of a gaunt old house, evidently let in lodgings.

Richmond Chartley, looking as charming as a handsome girl will look, in spite of a line of care upon her forehead and a twitch of anxiety upon the corners of her lips, was distributing coffee, and alternating the task by cutting bread-and-butter—thin-thick for her brother Hendon, who was reading a sporting paper, and thin-thin for Dr. Chartley, who was gazing in an abstracted manner at a paper before him, and making notes from time to time with a gilt pencil-case.

He was a bland-looking, handsome man, with stiff white cravat, and that suave, softly-smiling aspect peculiar to fashionable physicians; but the fashion had gone, though the smile remained, to be shed upon his two children instead of upon the patients who came no more.

The breakfast progressed, with Hendon eagerly taking in the details of the last Australian boat-race, and the doctor making a calculation for the variation of the compound that was the dream of his life, till, as it was finally ended, he bent forward, and said softly,

"Truly thankful, amen!"

Hendon Chartley rustled his paper, and doubled it up, and thrust it into his pocket.

"But no fried bacon," he said bitterly.

Dr. Chartley turned his beams upon his son, and shook his head slowly.

"Indigestible, Hendon. But never mind. Work as I do. Get to the top of the tree, and then you can keep your carriage, and destroy your liver with Strasburg pie."

"Bah!" said Hendon; but his father's countenance did not change.

"Going to the hospital, my boy?"

"Yes, the old dismal round."

"But to allay suffering. A great profession."

"Wish it had less profession and more solid satisfaction!" said the young man. "Good-by, Rich."

He hurried out of the room, and the next minute the door was heard to bang.

"An ornament to the profession some day, Richmond."

"Yes, dear, but—"

"Well, my love?" said the doctor, beaming upon her softly.

"Don't think me unkind, dear, now you are so deep in your study; but I do really want a little help."

"Certainly, my darling, certainly. Now, that's what I like; frank confidence on your part. You are the best of housekeepers, my child; but I don't want you to take all the burden on your shoulders."

Richmond Chartley sighed, and the line on her broad handsome forehead took to itself so many puckers, which, however, did not detract from her beauty.

"Well, my dear; speak out. You want something?"

"Yes, father; money."

"Ah!" said Dr. Chartley softly, as he tapped the table with the top of his worn pencil-case. "Money; you want money."

"Yes, father. I am horribly pressed. Poor Hendon has really not enough to pay for his lunch, and—"

"Yes, my dear; but Hendon will soon be in a position to provide comfortably for himself," said the doctor blandly.

The old proverb about the growing grass and the starving steed occurred to Richmond, but she only sighed.

"I don't think you need trouble yourself about Hendon, my dear."

"But there is the rent, father," said Richmond desperately, as the full extent of their position flashed upon her; and she felt impelled to speak.

"Ah, yes; the rent. I had forgotten the rent," said the doctor dreamily.

"Final and threatening notices have been left about the rates and taxes."

"Yes," said the doctor musingly. "The idea is Utopian, but I have often thought how pleasant life would be were there no rents or rates and taxes."

"Dear father, I must tell you all my troubles now I have begun," said Richmond, leaving her chair to kneel down before the handsome elderly man, and lay her hand upon his breast.

"Certainly, my darling, certainly," he said, bending down to kiss her brow in the most gentlemanly manner, and then caress her luxuriant hair.

"They have threatened to cut off both the gas and water."

"Tut! tut! how unreasonable, Richmond! Really a severe letter ought to be addressed to the companies' directors."

"And, father dear, the tradespeople are growing not only impatient, but absolutely insulting. What am I to do?"

"Wait, my darling, wait. Little clouds in our existence while we are attending the breaking forth of the sun. Not long, my dear. I am progressing rapidly with my discovery, and while I shall be content with the fame, you shall be my dear banker, and manage everything as you do now."

"Yes, yes, dear, I will; but it is so sad. No patients seem to come to you now."

"No, my dear, no," he replied calmly; "I'm afraid I neglected several, and they talked about it among themselves. These things will spread."

"Are there any means left of—pray forgive me, dear—of raising a little money?"

"No, my dear, I think not. But don't trouble about it. Any day now I may have my discovery complete, and then—but really, my dear, this is wasting time. I must get on with my work."

He rose, and Richmond sighed as with courtly grace he raised her hand and kissed it, smiling at her sadly and shaking his head.

"So like your dear mother," he said; "even to the tones of your voice. Don't let me be disturbed, Richmond. I am getting to a critical point."

He slowly crossed the room, gazing dreamily before him, and passed out, while his child stood listening to his step along the passage at the back of the sideboard till the door of the surgery was heard to close, when, clasping her hands, she gazed up at the Prince Regent, as if he were some kind of a fat idol, and exclaimed passionately,

"What shall I do? what shall I do?"

A violent twitch made her raise her hand to her face, which was contracted with pain, and she drew her breath hard; but the pang seemed to pass away, and after ringing the bell she began busily to pack the breakfast-things together.

Before she had half done, the door opened softly, and a rather dirty face was thrust in. It was the face of an old-looking boy with snub-nose, large mouth, and a rough, shock head bristling over his prominent forehead, and all redeemed by as bright and roguish-looking a pair of eyes as ever shone out from beneath a low type of head.

The door was only opened wide enough at first to admit the head, but as soon as its owner had given a glance round, the door opened farther, and the rest of a rather small person appeared, dressed in a well-worn page's button suit, partly hidden by a dirty green-baize bibbed apron.

The boy's sleeves were tucked up, and he was carrying a pair of old-fashioned Wellington boots by the tops, and these boots he held up on high.

"Didn't know, Miss, whether the doctor had gone. Been a-cleaning his boots. Look, Miss, there's a shine!"

"Yes, yes, Bob, they look very nice. Take them up-stairs, and then come and clear away."

"All right, Miss. I made a whole bottle o' blacking outer half a cake as a chap I knows give me."

"Yes, yes, Bob."

"Stunning blacking it is, too. He's in the Brigade, and I minded his box for him, and took sixpence while he went and had a game of marbles. That's why he give me the cake."

"Now, Bob, my good lad, I don't want to know anything about that. Take those boots up-stairs."

"All right, Miss; but do look how they shines. I polished tops and all. Look, Miss."

"Yes, yes, yes; they are beautifully clean."

"I allus thinks about legs, Miss, when I cleans boots; and when I thinks about legs, I think about the doctor making such a good job o' mine arter I was run over. It's stronger than the other; I am glad as it was broke."

"Glad?"

"Yes, Miss. Why, if I hadn't been run over, my leg wouldn't have been broke, and then the doctor wouldn't have mended it, and I shouldn't be here. What's she gone away for?" said the boy to himself, as he stared after Richmond. "She's been a-crying; one of her eyes was wet. What coward gals are to cry!"

The boy went to the door and listened, but all was perfectly still; so he set down the boots, rolled his apron into what he called a cow's tail, the process consisting in twisting it up very tightly and tucking it round his waist.

This done he listened again, and finding all still, he thrust his arms into the doctor's boots and indulged in a hearty laugh of a silently weird description before going down on all fours, and walking as slowly and solemnly round the table as a tom cat, whose movements he accurately copied, rubbing himself up against the legs of the table, and purring loudly.

This over, he rose to his feet and listened, but all being still; he went down upon all fours again and trotted round the table, leaped on to a chair, leaped down again, and ran out of the room and along the dark passage towards the head of the kitchen stairs, looking in the gloom wonderfully like some large ape.

Active as he was, a descent of the dark stone stairs on all fours was beyond him; so he rose up, and reaching over, glided silently down the balustrade, to the great detriment of his buttons. But, arrived upon the mat at the bottom, he once more resumed his quadrupedal attitude, thrust his hands well into the Wellington boots, and trotted with a soft patter into a dark back kitchen, out of which came a droning noise uttered by some one at work, and apparently under the impression that it was a song.

The boy, more animal-like than ever, disappeared in the gloom, with the boots making a low *pat-pat, pat-pat*, and then there was a loud shriek, and Bob bounded out, skimmed up the stairs, after evidently having alarmed some one, and disappeared with the boots, which he sedately carried up to the bedroom. Then descended, to listen at the head of the stairs to a complaining voice relating to Richmond Chartley an account of how an " ormuz " great dog had come down the area, run into the back kitchen, and frighted some one almost out of her wits!

Bob's face expressed happiness approaching the sublime, and he hurriedly cleared the breakfast-things, and took them down in time to be sent down by a not over clean-looking maid-of-all-work to shut that there gate.

The boy was in the act of performing this duty when a neatly-dressed girlish-looking body approached, carrying a large folio under one arm—a folio so broad that the neatly-mended and well-fitting little glove which covered a very small hand could hardly reach to the bottom.

"Is your mistress in?"

"Yes, Miss," said Bob, whose face seemed to reflect the sweet, sunny smile which greeted him. "I'll slip round and let you in."

"Oh!"

This was the utterance of the new arrival, as she saw the boy apparently hurl himself over the iron balustrade of the area-steps, and plunge into the dusthole region beyond. But Bob had long practised the keeping of his equilibrium as the polished state of the iron rail proved, and, instead of dashing out his brains on the stones, he reached the bottom with a bound, and diving into the house, reappeared in a marvelously short space of time at the front door.

"She's in the dining-room, Miss," said Bob, making a rush at the folio, and feasting his eyes the while on the natty fur-trimmed jacket and little furry hat, whose hue harmonized admirably with the wavy dark brown hair, neatly braided up beneath; for the visitor was remarkably well dressed, and her fresh young face set off everything so well that no one thought of noticing that the dress had been turned, and that the jacket's rough exterior had certainly last winter been upon the other side.

Bob hurriedly closed the door, and ran into the chilly dining-room with the folio, which he banged down on the table with—

"Here's Miss Heath, Miss;" and then darted out of the room, leaving the two girls face to face.

"They don't like me to see 'em cuddling," he said

with a grin; and, urged by the enormous amount of vitality that was in him, Bob bounded to the kitchen stairs to slide down, and directly after a gritty rubbing noise, made metrical to accompany the shrill whistling of a tune, arose, the result of the fact that Bob Hartnup, the doctor's boy, who clung to the house with the fidelity of a cat, was cleaning the knives.

Bob's facts were correct, if unrefined in expression, for the two girls flew to each other's arms, and as they kissed affectionately, each displayed tears in her eyes, while without relinquishing hands, they sat down together near the window.

"No news, Janet?" whispered Richmond.

Her visitor shook her head slowly, gazing wistfully the while into her companion's eyes.

"We must wait Rich dear. Africa is a horribly great place, and some day we shall hear that he is coming back."

Richmond Chartley made no reply, but sat gazing straight out through the uncleaned window, as if her large clear eyes were looking straight away over the ocean in search of the man she loved.

"Don't, don't, darling; don't look like that," whispered the younger girl. "Don't think all that again. It's cruel, it's wicked of them to have said such things. He was too young, and strong, and brave to die."

"Please God, yes!" said Richmond simply, but with a deep heart-stirring pathos in the tones of her rich voice.

"And one of these days he'll come, dear, like the good prince in the fairy tale, all rich and handsome, as my darling brother always was, and marry my own dear Rich, and make her happy again."

"Please God, yes!" said Richmond once more; and

this time there was resignation, and despair so plainly marked that her companion flung her arms about her neck and began to sob.

"Rich, dear Rich, don't, pray don't, or you'll drive me half mad. I've all my lessons to give to-day, and my hand will tremble, and I shall be so unnerved that I can do nothing."

"Janet dear, I try so hard not to despair, but the weary months roll by, and it is two years now since you have had a line."

"Yes, but what of that? Perhaps he is where there are no post-offices, or perhaps he is not getting on; and, poor boy, he is too proud to write till he is doing better. Why, he has only been away four years."

"Four years!" said Richmond sadly; "is it only four years?"

"That's all, dear, though it has seemed like eight, and we will not despair, even though it is so hard to bear. Why, Rich, I feel sometimes when I kneel down at night that if he were dead I should know it; he would not let us go on suffering if it were so."

"Janet dear, I feel sometimes as if it was wrong to have loved him."

"What, dear Mark?"

"Yes."

"Wrong? For shame! How could any girl who knew my darling old Mark as you did help loving him?"

"But it made him dissatisfied. I was the cause of his going away."

"That foolish thought again! You were not, dear. It would have been the same if he had loved any girl. He said that he would not ask any woman to be his wife while he was tied down here without any prospects; and he went off to make his fortune, as many another brave young Englishman has gone before."

"But I made him discontented, dear."

"You made him behave nobly. Why, what other man would have said as he did, 'I hold you to no engagement, I ask nothing of you: I only tell you that I love you with all my heart'?"

"'And some day I will return,'" said Richmond, in a low deep voice.

"Yes, and some day he will return, dear: I do believe it, I *will* believe it, and— Oh, Rich, Rich, Rich, why, why are we such unhappy girls?"

It was the elder's turn now to try and comfort the younger, who had burst into a passionate fit of weeping, so full of anguish that, at last, Richmond raised her friend's face, kissed it, and holding the bonny little head between her hands, she said, with almost motherly tenderness.

"Janet, Hendon has been speaking to you again?"

There was no reply.

"I knew it," said Richmond half angrily. "It was thoughtless and cruel of him!"

"No, no, don't blame him, dear. No one could be more noble and more good. You know how hard he works."

"Yes," said Richmond, with a sigh.

"And if he is impatient with his home and your father why, you must recollect that he is a man, and men are not meant to be patient and suffering like women."

"He is too thoughtless, Janet, and—I don't like to say it of my own brother—too selfish."

"No, no!" cried Janet, flushing.

"Yes, dear, yes. Could he have had his way, you

two would have been man and wife, and he half living on the earnings of these poor tiny little hands."

"I don't think he would have pressed me to it, Rich; and after all, it was because he loved me so."

"Yes, and would have taken advantage of your loneliness here in this great cruel city, and dragged you down to poverty and misery such as I am bearing now. Janet, Janet dear, I feel sometimes as if I cannot bear this miserable degradation longer, and that all these troubles must be a punishment for my not telling my father about Mark."

"Why, Rich," said Janet, turning comforter once more, "what was there to tell? You made no engagement. And look here, if so much trouble is to come of love, why, you and I will take vows, and be single all our days. There, now, you look more like yourself; and I'm going to tell you my news."

"News?" cried Richmond, starting eagerly, and then looking sadly at her friend.

"Yes, two more pupils. I'm getting along famously now. And it does make me so happy and resigned. There, I must go, but—"

"You have something more to say to me?"

"Yes, only—there, I will be firm. Don't be angry with me, Rich dear, for I seem to have no one to care for here but you, and some day you shall pay me again, and I want you to borrow this."

She slipped a tiny little purse into Richmond's hands, and then turned scarlet, as she saw her companion's pallid face.

"No, no, Janet, I could not: your little scraped together earnings. Pray don't speak to me like that again."

"I must. I will!" cried the girl, with passionate

earnestness. "I don't want it, dear, and it is only a loan. Do, do, pray take it."

"I could not," said Richmond, thrusting the purse into her friend's hand.

"For Mark's sake, dear."

"For Mark's sake!" faltered Richmond hoarsely.

"Yes; how could I look him in the face again, if I had not behaved to you as he bade me when we said good-by on board the ship?"

"As he bade you?"

"Yes; to be as a sister to you always, and to look to you as a sister for help and comfort when I was in need. Yes, dear, for Mark's sake."

For answer, Richmond Chartley took her friend once more in her arms, and kissed her, but only to press the purse back into her hand before going with her to the door, from which they both shrank on opening it, for a loud voice exclaimed,

"Thank you! How do? Ah! Miss Chartley, is the doctor within?"

CHAPTER III.

THE DOCTOR AT HOME.

"YES, my father is at home, Mr. Poynter," said Richmond, speaking calmly, and drawing back for the visitor to enter.

Then to Janet, in a whisper.

"Can you stay with me a few minutes?"

"I daren't, dear; I am late now, and— Yes, I understand. I will."

It was Richmond's turn to display her firmness, and mastering a nervous trepidation which she felt, she bent down, kissed her friend, and, with a meaning pressure of the hand, said "good-by," and ushered the fresh visitor, who was busily turning a crimson silk handkerchief round a painfully glossy hat, into the dining-room.

"Thankye," he said, sitting down, but jumping up again, and placing another chair, "beg pardon, won't you sit down? I'm in no hurry if the doctor's engaged."

He nervously seized a very thick gold chain, and dragged a great gold watch from his pocket to consult.

"Eleven," he said; "thought I'd come and see him as I went into the City. Nothing the matter, much, but it's as well to see your medical man."

"I'll tell my father you are here, Mr. Poynter."

"No, don't hurry. I'm very busy at my place, but plenty of time, how's Hendon."

"My brother is quite well."

"Is he, now? That's right. Fine thing, good health, ain't it?"

"Of course," said Richmond quietly.

"Yes, of course; so it is, Miss Chartley. Hendon always seems to be a fine strong fellow. I always liked him since I met him at a fellow's rooms. Not at home now?"

"Oh, no; he has gone on to the hospital."

"Ah, yes. Feel sometimes as if I should go to the hospital."

The visitor appeared to be a florid, strongly-built man, in the most robust health, save that probably a love of too many of the good things of this life had made its mark upon him.

"I will tell my father you are here, said Richmond again; and this time she escaped from the room, to come suddenly upon Bob outside, striking an attitude indictive of a determination to crush the glossy hat left upon the table in the hall; and so sudden was Richmond's appearance that the boy stood fast, as if struck with catalepsy, for a few seconds before he bethought himself of a way out of his difficulty, when, pretending to catch a fly which did not exist, he turned upon his heel, and beat an ignominous retreat to the lower regions.

Dr. Chartley's patient was no sooner left alone than he started up, and began smoothing his short, carefully-parted hair, took off a second glove to display half a dozen jewelled rings, and wetting fingers and thumbs, he twirled the begummed points of his moustache, and fell into a state of agitation about the cut of his ultra-fashionably made clothes.

He looked round in vain, for there was no looking-glass; still, he had some satisfaction, for he was able to see that his tightly-fitting patent-leather boots were spotless, and that the drab gaiters with pearl buttons were exactly in their places; though the largely-checked trousers he wore did give him trouble as to the exact direction the outer seams should take, whilst his sealskin vest would look spotty in certain lights.

He was in the act of re-smoothing his hair when Richmond returned, and, hard City man as he was, he could not avoid an increase of depth in his color as he saw that the handsome woman before him was watching him intently.

"My father will come to you directly, Mr. Poynter," she said quietly.

"Oh, all right; but don't let me drive you away, Miss Chartley. I don't see much society, and chat's pleasant sometimes, ain't it?"

"Of course," said Richmond quietly; "but I thought my brother said you were fond of society."

"Fond of it? yes, of course," said Poynter hastily; and he smoothed his double fringe over his forehead again, where the hairdresser had cut it into a pattern which he had assured him was in the height of fashion, but only with the result of making him look like a butcher turned betting-man. "Yes, fond of it," he said again, "and of course I can get plenty with fellows, but—er—ladies' society is what I like."

James Poynter directed at Richmond a smiling leer, one which had proved very successful at more than one metropolitan bar, where he had paved the way for its success with gifts of flowers and a cheap ring or two; but it was utterly lost here, for its intended recipient was looking another way, and as it faded from its inventor's face there was a blank, inane expression left, bordering upon the grotesque.

"You should go more into ladies' society, then, Mr. Poynter, as soon as your health permits," said Richmond, with provoking coolness.

"Oh, I'm not ill," he said hastily; and his forehead grew damp as he floundered about, looking fishy now about the eyes and mouth, which opened and shut at intervals, as if to give passage to words which never came. "Felt I was—er—little out of sorts, you know, and thought I'd see the doctor. Let's see, I said so before, didn't I?"

"Yes, I think you did, Mr. Poynter. Here is my father."

There was a slight cough just then, the door opened, and the doctor entered, his bland, aristocratic presence contrasting broadly with that of his patient.

"Ah, Poynter," he said, "good-morning. Don't

go, my dear; Mr. Poynter will come into my consulting-room, I daresay."

"Yes, of course," cried the patient, shaking hands, and forgetting to leave off. "I shall—shall you?—good-morning, Miss Chartley."

He released the doctor's hand, to turn and shake Richmond's which he pressed desperately, and then followed the bland, calm, stately doctor out of the room, when he caught up his hat savagely and ground his teeth in the dark passage.

"I feel just like a fool when I'm with her!" he said to himself. "I never feel so anywhere else. And I ain't a fool. I should just like to see the man who would say I was."

The doctor led the way through the glazed door into the dim surgery, with its rows of bottles, and stoppered glass jars containing unpleasant looking specimens preserved in spirits, all carefully labelled and inscribed in the doctor's own neat hand, but grown yellow with time; and as he closed the door after his patient, the latter's nostrils distended slightly, and an air of disgust chased the inane look as he breathed the unpleasant medicinal druggy air.

"I was just busy over my discovery," continued the doctor blandly, "and I thought as a friend you would not mind coming here—it is the consulting-room, my dear Poynter; and I could go on, and we could chat over your ailment the while."

"Oh, it's all the same to me," said Poynter; and, once out of Richmond's presence, he seemed another being. Instead of carrying his glossy hat in his hand, he had resumed it, and wore it with a vulgar cock; he walked with the swagger of the low-class City man; and his face shone as he whisked out a second crimson silk handkerchief redolent of perfume, and blew his nose with a loud blast, which sounded defiant.

"Here we are," said the doctor, smiling at his patient, as if after a long search he had found the ill which troubled him, and pulled it up by the roots. "Take that chair, my dear Poynter," he continued, pointing to one by the fire, where a bright copper kettle was on the hob, and closing the door, while his patient took off his hat, glanced round the room, and blew the dust off the top of a side table before depositing thereon his new head-covering.

There was a litter on the table, a chemist's set of weights and scales, divers papers, a spatula, pestle and mortar of glass, toy-like in size, and a book with memoranda, and pen and ink.

"Very busy, you see, Poynter; I've nearly completed my task, and in a few months, perhaps weeks, the medical world will be startled by my discovery."

"What are you going to do with it when you've done?"

"Do with it?"

"Yes. Now, if I was you, I should say to a friend, 'Lend me a thou.,' and then take a little shop, put it up in bottles, with threehalfpenny stamps, and advertise it well as the new patent medicine."

"My dear Mr. Poynter!"

"Hold hard, doctor, I haven't done," he cried, speaking in a hard, browbeating manner, as if he were giving orders. "Give it a spanking name, 'Heal-all,' or 'Cure all;' won't do to say Kill-all, eh? Haw, haw, haw!"

He burst into a coarse, loud laugh, and the doctor sank back in his chair, with his brows twitching slightly.

"Hold hard, I have it. Nothing like a good name for the fools who swallow everything. Get something out of one of your Greek and Latin physic books—one of those words like hippocaustus or allegorus, or something they can't understand."

"I do not quite see the force of your argument, my dear Mr. Poynter," said the doctor blandly.

"Not see? Why, man, it would be patent medicine then, and no one could take it from you. Look at Hannodyne—good stuff, too, when you've got a headache in the morning—Government stamp, to imitate which is forgery!"

"But still, I—"

"Don't see? Nonsense! Make a fortune. You want it. Patients pretty scarce, eh?"

He laughed again offensively, and the doctor winced, but kept up his bland smooth smile.

"And suppose I took your advice, my dear Poynter, where is the friend to lend me a thousand pounds?"

"Ah! where's the friend!" said Poynter, with a meaning look. "P'r'aps I know the friend, if things went as he wanted."

The doctor's face changed slightly, but his visitor was too obtuse to see it.

"And would you suggest that I should—er—preside in the little shop and sell the allegorus?"

"Ah, that ain't a bad name, is it?" said Poynter, giving his head a shake in the stiff collar in which it rested as an egg does in a cup. "No, not you; not business-like enough. Make Hendon do that."

"Ah," said the doctor slowly, as he took up the bottle, removed the stopper, and smelled the contents before moistening one finger and tasting it.

"You'll end by poisoning yourself with that stuff, doctor," said Poynter, chuckling.

"No," he said blandly, "no, my dear James Poynter, no; it is a life-giver, not a destroyer. Now, if you were to take, say, twenty drops in water—"

"With sugar?" said Poynter, grinning.

"Yes, with sugar, if you liked. There's no objection to flavoring the vehicle—water."

"Vehicle—water? Why, I never heard of water being called a vehicle! Thought vehicle meant a carriage or trap."

"In this case the water would be the vehicle, Poynter, and, as I was saying, if you were to take twenty drops of this extract, or rather, compound, you would feel as if a new lease of life were beginning—that everything looked brighter; that nerve and muscle were being strung up; your power of thought greater, and—try a little, my dear sir."

"No, thankye, doctor; but if you've got a drop of brandy in the place and a bottle of soda, you may make it more than twenty drops of that."

"I have some brandy," said the doctor, rising, "but no soda-water. I can mix you a little soda and tartaric acid, though, in a glass of water, and it will have all the effect."

James Poynter showed his great white teeth in a broad grin, threw himself back in the patients' chair, and unhooking his watch-chain, began to swing round the big seal, pencil-case, and sovereign-purse which hung at the end.

"No, thankye, doctor," he said. "Let's have the brandy-and-water, and sugar purissima, as you folks call it now, and you can mix me up a tonic and send it on."

"Certainly, my dear Poynter, certainly," said the doctor, going to a closet, and taking out a spirit decanter, tumbler, and sugar, which he placed upon the stained green-baize table-cover, smilingly looking on afterwards with a little bright copper kettle in his hand as his visitor poured out liberally into his glass.

"All right, eh, doctor?" said the young man, looking up in the bland, smooth face, with a good many wrinkles about his right eye.

"I—er—do not understand you."

"Brandy all right? No pilly-cosky or anything of that sort in it? Fill right up."

"No," said the doctor, smiling. "It's the best brandy, and I'll take a little with you."

He filled up his guest's glass, and then smilingly took a second tumbler from the cupboard, and mixed himself a draught.

"Yes, not bad brandy, doctor, but wants age," said Poynter, rinsing his mouth with the hot spirit and water, as if he had been cleaning his teeth. "Now, I have a few dozen of a fine old cognac in my cellar that would give this fifty in a hundred, and lick it hollow."

Perhaps to be expressive, Mr. James Poynter shuffled his shoulders against the cushion of the chair and licked his lips, ending with a fish-like smack.

"Let me send you a dozen, doctor."

"No, no, my dear sir. I did not know you were in the wine and spirit trade."

"Stuff and nonsense!"

"And I could not afford—"

"Yah! Who asked you to? I meant as a present. Wine and spirit trade, indeed! Hang it! Do I look like a publican?"

Dr. Chartley told an abominable lie, for if ever man, from the crown of his pomatumed head, down over his prominent nubbey forehead, small eyes, prominent cheekbones, unpleasant nose, and heavy jaw, to the toes of his boots, looked like a fast, race-attending licensed victualler, it was James Poynter.

Dr. Chartley said, in answer to the indignant question, "No."

"Humph!" ejaculated the visitor, mollifying himself with a large draught of brandy-and-water. "I should think not, indeed. I shall send you a dozen of that brandy."

"No, no, I beg!" said the doctor earnestly; and his white forehead puckered up.

"Yes, I shall. May I smoke?"

"Certainly—certainly."

A very large, well-filled cigar case was already in the visitor's hands.

"Take one."

"No, thanks. I never smoke."

"Never mind, Hendon does. Here, I shall leave those six for him."

"I really would rather you did not, Poynter; indeed I would."

"Get out! What's the good of having these things if some one else don't enjoy 'em too? Make Hendon a bit more civil to me. He is so jolly—so jolly—what do you call it?—soopercilious with me. Because I'm not a doctor, I suppose. There's half a dozen good ones for him when he comes in. Now, then, doctor, go ahead. Want to see my tongue?"

"No—no," said the doctor; "the look of your eye

is sufficient, Mr. Poynter. It is much clearer. Felt any more of the chest symptoms?"

"No, not so much of them; but I don't sleep as I should: feverish and tossy—spend half my nights punching my pillow."

"Have you given up the suppers?"

"Well, not quite. You see a man can't drop everything. I know a lot of men, and one's obliged, you see, to do as they do. But now look here; doctor. You've been treating me these three months."

"Dear me! is it so long as that?"

"More. You've poked my chest about, and listened to my works, and given me all sorts of stuff to take, and told me to eat this and drink that, and now I suppose you think I'm sound, wind and limb?"

"Certainly, my dear sir, certainly. I told you so at the first, and that no treatment was necessary."

"Yes, yes, all right; but I'd got to be a bit nervous, doctor, and now, as I say, you think me sound, wind and limb?"

"Quite."

"Then you'll agree, wont you?"

"Agree?" said the doctor, looking over the glasses he had put on when commencing to be professional.

"Yes. I'm as good a man as there is at Mincing Lane over a tea bargain; but a job like this knocks the wind out of me, makes me feel a damaged lot where the sea-water's got in, or a Maloo mixture. Can't do it: but you understand."

"Really, Mr. Poynter, I—"

"Now don't run away, doctor; don't, please. I'm a warm man, and I'm getting warmer. My house is tip-top. I gave two-fifty for the piano, I did, 'pon my soul, and fifty apiece for the cut-glass chandies in the drawing-room. There ain't a better garden in Sydenham. You're willing, ain't you?"

"Do you mean—"

"Yes, that's it. Say the word. There, I've loved her ever since I first saw her. And situated as you are, doctor—"

"Mr. Poynter.

"No offence meant—far from it; but of course I can't help seeing how things are. Come, you'll give your consent, and get hers, and I'll make settlements —anything you like. You shall come and have a bit o' dinner with us every Sunday, and a glass o' real port wine; and if you'd rather have a cab to come home, why, there you are. Come, there's my hand. Where's yours?"

"Do I understand—"

"Stop a moment, doctor. Of course you'll attend us, whether we're ill or whether we ain't. Keep us in order, like; and as to your fees, why, I ask you now, as a man, what *is* a fee to me?"

"Mr. Poynter!"

"One moment, doctor. I don't say anything about a brougham. If Miss Richmond— I say, doctor, what made you call her Richmond and him Hendon?"

"A foolish whim—eccentricity," said the doctor coldly. "One child was born on the North Road, the other at the pretty old place on the south west."

"I see. Well, as I was saying, if Miss Richmond likes it to be a brougham, either the real thing, or on the job, she has only got to speak, and it's hers."

"Am I to understand, Mr. Poynter, that this is a formal proposal for my daughter's hand?"

"That's it. How you can put it, doctor! You're right; it is, and there's my hand."

"Mr. Poynter," said the doctor, drawing himself up in his chair, and without taking the extended hand, "that is a matter upon which I am not prepared to speak."

"Why, you're her father, ain't you?"

"Does my daughter sanction this?"

"Well—er—yes—no—hardly, because I've never put it to her plump. But you know what women are—sealskins, a carriage, bit o' jewelry, and their own way. Why, of course she does; did you ever know a woman as didn't want to marry? They often say so, but— You know. There, say the word: I'll just go in and see her, and it'll be a good job for all of us, and I shall go away with the day fixed."

"No, Mr. Poynter," said the doctor gravely; "I have been a medical man for thirty years—a great student, but I must frankly confess that I do not know what women are. As to my daughter, she is of an age to judge for herself, and when she accepts a man for her husband—"

"I say, hold hard; there's nothing on, is there?"

"You have told me that you love my child."

"Like all that, doctor. But you know what I mean: old lover, priory attachment, and that sort of thing."

"As far as I know, there has never been any attachment. Richmond is not like most girls."

"Right doctor. She isn't. That fetched me. Why, in her plain shabby things—"

The doctor winced.

"She knocks my sister into fits, and Lyddy spends two-fifty a year in dressmaking and millinery, without counting jewelry and scent."

"I may say," continued the doctor, "that my daughter has always devoted herself to her brother and me."

"Oh, yes, doctor, I've spotted that," said the visitor, smoking furiously.

"And I have never seen any sign of an attachment. I once thought that there was a liking between her and young Mark Heath."

"What, brother to that Miss Janet who comes here?" cried Poynter eagerly.

"The same; but that was years ago."

"And he's abroad, isn't he?"

"He went to the Cape—to seek his fortune," said the doctor gravely; "but he has not been heard of now for two years."

"Dead, safe!" said Poynter, drawing a breath full of relief.

"I'm afraid so."

"Afraid?"

"It would be sad if the young man had ended his career like that."

"Of course. But they weren't engaged?"

"Certainly not, Mr. Poynter."

"And you've no objection to me, doctor?"

"N-no—I—that is, Mr. Poynter, "I look upon this as a matter for my daughter to decide."

"Of course, doctor. Well, I'll just finish my cigar and grog, and then I'll go and put it to her, plump and plain; and, as I said before, it'll be a fine day's work for us all.

The doctor sighed.

"I say, you know," continued his visitor, with the wrinkles coming about his eyes, "it was all a dodge o' mine."

"I beg your pardon."

"There wasn't anything the matter with me when I came."

"Nothing whatever," said the doctor, nodding acquiescence.

"What! you knew that?"

"Of course I did. I looked upon it as all imaginary."

"But you took the fees, doctor?" said the young man laughing.

"You took up my time."

"But I say, doctor, isn't that too bad?"

"Not at all. My dear sir, the medical profession would be a poor one if we had no patients with imaginary ills. We treat them; they think we do them good; and they grow better. Surely we earn our fees."

"Oh, but, doctor," said the young man jocularly, "why not honestly tell them they are all right, instead of taking their coin?"

"Because if we did they would not believe us, and would go to some other medical man."

"Then you knew I was all right?"

"Certainly I did."

"And made me up that wretched physic to take."

"You would not have been satisfied without."

"Ah, well," said the young man, with a chuckle which resulted in his wiping his eyes with his highly scented handkerchief, "I never took a drop"

"I know that too," said the doctor.

"Ah, well; we understand one another now, and I'd better go."

James Poynter, however. seemed to be in no hurry to go, but sipped his brandy-and-water, smoked his cigar down to the throwing-away length, and then brought out from his vest-pocket an amber and meerschaum mouthpiece, tipped with gold, into which he fitted the wet end of the cigar, and smoked till he could smoke no longer, when he rose, flush-faced, and with the dew upon his forehead.

"I suppose I must go and get it done, doctor," he said; "but it's rather a—well, it makes a man feel— I say, doctor, what is there in a pretty woman that makes a man feel half afraid of her, like?"

"I told you, Mr. Poynter, a short time back, that I did not understand women," said the doctor gravely. "I cannot tell. Say Nature's heaven-gift for her defence."

"Humph!" said Poynter, staring. "I say, doctor —cigar, you know. Could you give a fellow a mouthful of something that would take the taste out of one's mouth? Going to see a lady."

"Try cold water," said the doctor, in a tone of voice which sounded like throwing that fluid upon the young man's hopes; but he had so much faith in himself that the verbal water glanced from his fine feathers, and after rinsing his mouth, he shook hands clumsily, intending to leave the doctor's fee within his palm, but managed to drop the more valuable of the two coins on the edge of the fender, when it flew beneath the grate, and had to be fished out with the tongues.

"Dodgy stuff, money, doctor," said Poynter, setting down the fire-iron, and blowing the coin.

"Don't take all that trouble, pray."

"Oh, it's no trouble, doctor. I was never above picking up a sov. There, don't you come. I know my way;" and he left the consulting-room to go into the house and learn his fate.

"Brute!" said the doctor, with a look of disgust, as he sank into his chair. "Why is Fate so unfair with her gold! I thought as much, but Richmond will say *no*."

"Old lunatic!" said James Poynter, with his fat upper lip curling in disgust, as his eyes lit on the row of glass jars with their ghastly contents. "Once I get my lady home, I don't mean to see much of him. Here, boy," he said, as he reached the hall, and so suddenly that there was nearly a serious accident, for Bob was coming down the balustrade from the first floor, gliding upon the central part of his person with arms and legs extended—taking hold having grown common.

The sharp "Here, boy!" so startled him that he overbalanced himself, went right over, but caught at the upright spindly bars, and so far saved himself that he came down upon his feet in a couple of somersaults, recovering himself directly, and coming forward with a grin upon his bloodless face, as if the feat had been intended.

"Ah, you'll break your neck some day. Here's a shilling for you. Take me into Miss Chartley at once."

Bob bit the coin, and slipped it into his pocket before he replied,

"Gone out."

"Gone out? Will she be long?"

"Dessay she'll be hours, sir."

James Poynter stamped with his foot, and muttered something unparliamentary.

"Tell Miss Chartley," he said. "No, don't tell her anything. Here, let me out."

Bob ran to the ponderous old door, and

holding it open with his eyes glittering as he stared at the visitor, till he had hurried out with his hat set very much on one side, and walked sharply away.

"Thought he'd want the bob again," said the boy. 'Just do for the old gal. Well, I'm blessed!"

This last consequent upon his catching sight of a shabby-looking figure in black, with a damaged bonnet, and a weirdly dissipated look, rising slowly into sight up the area-steps, and then coming out of the creaking gate to the boy, who grew more serious the nearer the figure came.

It was not a pleasant face to look upon, for it was not over-clean; the black and gray hair was ill-arranged, and the eyes that shone above the flushed cheeks belied the woman sadly if they did not tell the truth about potations.

"Why, Bob, my darling," she said, with an exaggerated fawning smile, "and how is my bonny boy?"

"Here stow that, mother," cried the lad, struggling from an embrace. "Don't! Can't yer see I've been brushing my hair?"

"Yes, and it looks beautiful, ducky. I've been knocking ever so long at the hairy door, and that fine madam saw me, and wouldn't let me in."

"No; she says I ain't never to let you in no more."

"Not let me in no more to see my own boy?"

"No; she says you took some fresh butter last time you was here, and you sha'n't come."

"Then you sha'n't stay, Bob; I'll take you away, my darling. Oh, it's a wicked, cruel world!"

"Here, I say, mother, stow that. Whatcher want?"

"Want, my darling? Yes, that's it: want—staring want; but you sha'n't stay here."

"Get out! I shall."

"No, you sha'n't, you ungrateful boy. I won't be separated from my own child. Bob dear, have you got any money?"

"Eh?"

"Anybody give you anything?" whined the woman. "There ain't been nothing pass my lips this blessed day."

"Oho! what a wunner!" cried the boy. "Why, I can smell yer."

"No, no, my dear; that's Mrs. Billson as you can smell. I've been talking to her, and she drinks 'orrid. Ain'tcher got a few pence for your poor lone mother, who's ready to break her heart sometimes because she's parted from her boy?"

"Will you go away if I give you something?"

"Go away? Oho!" whined the woman, wiping off a maudlin tear with the end of her shawl.

"Here, I say, don't cry on the front doorsteps. Come down in the hairy, where nobody can't see you."

"Driven away by my own boy! Oho, oho!"

"'Tain't my fault. Doctor said you wasn't to come, and if you did he'd send me away."

"Then come home, Bob, to your poor heartbroken mother."

"Walker!" cried the boy. "Why yer ain't got no home to give a chap."

"No home?"

"Well, I don't call that a home, living up in a hattic along o' old Mother Billson."

"Oh, you ungrateful boy! Ain't it enough for me to have come down so that I'm obliged to see my own son in liveries, without him turning against me."

"Who's a-turning again you? Don't cry, I tell yer," he said, angrily stamping a foot.

"Then you shall come home."

"Sha'n't. I ain't going to leave the doctor and Miss Rich for nobody, so there"

"Ugh, you viper!"

"Here, stow that. Who's a viper? See what they've done for me when I was runned over. Why, if it hadn't been for Miss Rich a-nussing of me when you was allus tipsy, you wouldn't have had no boy at all, only a dead 'un berrid out at Finchley along o' the old man."

"Ah, you wicked ungrateful little serpent! They've been setting you again your poor suffering mother."

"Stow that, I say. You'll have the doctor hear you if you don't be quiet."

"I won't be quiet, you wicked, wicked—"

"Look here! If you don't hold your row, I won't give you the bob and two coppers I've got for you."

"Have you got some money for your poor mother, then?"

"I've got a bob a gent give me, and twopence, my half of what we got for the bones me and 'Lisbeth sold."

"Ah! I'm a poor suffering woman, and I do say things sometimes as I don't mean," whined the wretched creature. "Give me the money, dear, and let me go."

"If I give it to yer, you won't say no more about my coming away?"

"No, dear; I only want to see you happy."

"Well, there, then," he said, giving her the coins; "and, I say—"

"Yes, my precious."

"You ain't to spend none of it in gin."

"Gin? Oh, no, my dear."

"Get some pudding out of Holborn, and a saveloy; and, I say, mother, get yourself a bit o' tea."

"Yes my darling."

"And don't let Mrs. Billson gammon you into lending her none of it."

"No, my dear. And there, good-by, Bob; be a good-boy. I won't come wherriting of you no more'n I can help."

The miserable object, from whom out of compassion Richmond Chartley had rescued the boy, shuffled along the street to the nearest public-house, to buy more plus spirit with which to attack her miserable minus spirit, with the result that, as a mathematical problem, one would kill the other as sure as Fate.

Meanwhile Bob stood on the step watching her.

"Wonder whether the old gal does like me? Somehow she allus goes as soon as she gets all a chap's got. Now she'll go and have a drop. She allus does when she says she won't."

"Bob! you Bob!" came in a shrill voice from the kitchen stairs.

"Can't you see I'm a coming?" cried the boy; and hurriedly closing the door, he returned to his work.

CHAPTER IV.

PUBLIC OPINION ON CURRENT EVENTS.

THERE was a desperate scuffle going on round the corner as Hendon Chartley came by one day, and he would have passed on without seeing it, only that his English blood was stirred at the way in which the odds were all on one side—four boys being engaged in pummelling one who, in spite of the thrashing he was getting, fought on boldly, till, with a couple of sharp cuts of his cane, Hendon settled two of the combatants, when the other two ran away.

"Thankye, sir."

"You young dog, is it you?" cried Hendon.

"Yes, sir; and I should ha' licked all on 'em if you hadn't come."

"Why, you ungrateful young rascal, be off back and wash your face. Look here: I'll have you turned away."

"No, sir; please, sir, don't, sir. I couldn't help it, sir. I was obliged to fight, sir; I was indeed, sir. Oh, don't, sir; you hurts!"

Hendon listened to no remonstrance, but catching the boy by the collar he thrust him back till he reached the door, which he opened with his latch-key, and, bundling the boy in, sent him staggering along the hall as he closed the door, and went on once more.

"Yah! who cares for you?" cried the boy angrily; and then his countenance changed, and he broke into a smile as he found himself face to face with Rich.

"Why, Bob," she exclaimed, "what is the matter?"

"I couldn't help it, Miss. Mr. Hendon shoved me in like that. I meant to come in by the area."

"But why did he bring you back like that? Did he know where you had been?"

"Oh, no, Miss! I never tells anybody where I'm going with a note for you; not even Mr. Poynter, Miss. Here's the letter; and Miss Heath said I was to give her love to you, and she hadn't been because she was so busy."

Bob drew a letter from his pocket, and as he did so made upon it an ugly mark.

"Why, Bob, your hand's bleeding!"

"Is it, Miss? Oh, ah! so it is That ain't nothink."

"You are all over mud, too. Have you met with an accident again?"

The boy's lips parted to say "*Yes*," but as he gazed up into the clear searching eyes which looked down so kindly into his, he shook his head.

"No, Miss," he said boldly.

"Why, Bob, you have not been fighting?"

"1 didn't want to fight, Miss; but what's a chap to do?"

"Surely not fight when he is sent on an errand," said Rich severely.

"I didn't want to fight," said the boy again: "but I was fighting', and Mr. Hendon ketched me."

"I'm afraid, Bob, I shall be obliged to speak to my father, and have you sent away."

"No, no! don't do that, Miss; please don't. I will be so very useful, and I will do everythink 'Lisbeth tells me. Don't send a feller away."

"We cannot keep a boy who behaves so badly," continued Rich, who was trying to hide being amused and pleased at the boy's affectionate earnestness.

"Then I won't fight no more," said Bob. "But you don't know what it is, Miss. You don't know how the fellers tease yer. They're allers at yer. Soon as yer goes down the street, some one shouts 'Bottles!' Jest because I takes out the physic. I should jest like to make some on 'em take it. I'd give 'em a dose."

"But, Bob, you ought to be too sensible to take any notice about a rude boy calling you names."

"So I am, Miss," cried the boy, "ever so much. I never did nothing till they began on the doctor."

"Began on the doctor?"

"Yes, Miss; saying all sorts o' things about him. I shouldn't like to tell you what."

"And I should not like to hear, Bob," said Rich gravely, as she went up-stairs; while after waiting till he heard a door close, Bob went cautiously into the surgery, crept to the door of the consulting-room, and listened to find out whether the doctor was there, and finding him absent, the boy went nimbly to the nest of drawers, opened one, and took out a pair of scissors before lifting a tin case from a corner— a case which looked like the holder of a map.

Bob removed the lid, drew out a roll of diachylon, and after cutting off a strip, he replaced the lid and scissors, and descended to the kitchen, were Elizabeth was peeling potatoes, and making the droning noise which she evidently believed to be a song.

"Look ye here!" cried the boy, triumphantly showing his bleeding knuckles.

Elizabeth uttered a faint cry.

"Why, you've been fighting!" she cried. "Oh, you bad wicked boy!"

"So are you," cried Bob tauntingly: "you'd fight if the chaps served you as they did me, and said what they did about the doctor."

"What did they say?" said the girl, giving her nose a rub as if to make it more plastic.

"You bathe them cuts nistely and put some sticking-plaister on, and I'll tell you."

Elizabeth set down the potato basin, wiped her

hands, and after filling a tin bowl full of cold water, and fetching a towel, she tenderly bathed the boy's dirty injured hands.

"Now tell me what they said about the doctor," she said coaxingly.

"Why, they gets saying things to try and get me took away. My old woman don't like me stopping."

"She's a dreadful old creature," said Elizabeth angrily, "and I won't have her here."

"So's your old woman a dreadful old creature," retorted Bob, "and I won't have her here."

"My mother's been dead ten years," said Elizabeth, battling with an obstinate bit of mud, "and I won't have you speak to me in that impudent way."

"Then you leave my poor old woman alone."

"You let her stop away instead of always coming down them area-steps, and you encouraging her."

"That I don't, so come now. She's my old woman and I'm very fond on her; but I wish she wouldn't come. She allus comes when I'm busy."

"And she ought to be very glad you are here."

"But she ain't. She says doctors are bad 'uns, and that they do all sorts o' things as they oughtn't to. She was in the orspittle once, and she said it was horrid, and if she hadn't made haste and got well they'd have 'sected her."

"Lor!" said Elizabeth, drying the boy's hands with a series of gentle pats of the towel.

"And she says she knows the doctor does them sort o' things on the sly, and that she shall take me away, and I don't want to go."

"Well, that didn't make you fight, did it?"

"Yes, it did, now. I was going to tell you, on'y you're in such a hurry. I went to take a letter for

Miss Rich this morning, and as I was coming back, I meets mother, and she was asking me if I'd got any—"

"Money?" said Elizabeth promptly.

"Well, s'pose she did? If your mother warn't dead, and hadn't any money, p'r'aps if she met you in the street she'd ask you for money. Then how would you like it if four chaps come and said, 'Hallo, Bottles, how many dead 'uns have you got in the dust-hole?"

"Lor! did they say that?" said Elizabeth, squeezing the boy's hand in the interest she took.

"I say don't! You hurt. Here, cut up some o' that dacklum and warm it, and stick it on. Then one on 'em said he looked through the keyhole one day, and saw the doctor sharpening his knife; and that set mother off crying, and she sets down on a door-step, and goes on till she made me wild; and the more she cried and said she'd take me away the more they danced about, and called me body-snatcher."

"How awful!" said Elizabeth, holding a strip of diachylon at the end of the scissors to warm at the fire.

"But I got the old woman off at last for twopence, and soon as she'd gone I was coming home, and I met them four again, and they began at me once more."

"Did they, though?" said Elizabeth.

"Yes, and I pitched into 'em; and so would any one, I say. Why, it's enough to make the old woman fetch me away. I say, Liz, you don't want me to go, do you?"

"Indeed, but I do, sir."

"No, you don't. I ay, Liz, I'm so precious hungry. Got anything to give a fellow?"

"No. You took out two slices of bread and dripping to eat as you went."

Bob nodded.

"Why you never went and give them to that old woman, did you?"

"Ah, your mother's been dead ten years," said Bob sententiously. "S'pose I did give it to her? It was mine, and I wasn't obliged to eat it, was I? Thankye, that'll do."

Bob patted the plaister down on his knuckles, and had reached the kitchen door, when Elizabeth of the smudgy face called him by name, and, with as near an approach to a smile as she could display, showed him a piece of pudding on the cupboard shelf.

"And you said you wanted me to go," said Bob, with his mouth full, after a busy pause; "but I know'd you didn't mean it. I say, Liz, is that big gent with the rings and chains and shiny hat going to marry Miss Rich?"

"I don't know," said Elizabeth, suddenly growing deeply interested. "Why?"

"Because he's always coming to see the doctor, and whenever I let him in he asks me where Miss Rich is, and gives me something."

"Lor!"

"Yes, and he looks at her so."

"Do he, now? And what does Miss Rich say?"

"Oh, she only talks to him about its being fine or rainy, and as if she didn't want to stop in the room."

"Then she is," said Elizabeth triumphantly.

"Is? Is what?"

"Going to marry him. That's the proper way for a lady to behave."

"Oh!" said Bob shortly, and a curious frown came over his countenance. "I don't like him, somehow. I wish one didn't want money quite so bad."

Bob went up-stairs, and the place being empty he shut himself up in the surgery, to indulge in a morbid taste for trying flavor or odor of everything in the place, and fortunately so far without fatal or even dangerous results.

After a time he had a fit, and prescribed for himself *Syrup Aurantii*—so much in cold water, leaving himself in imagination in the chair while he mixed the medicine, and going back to the chair to take it. After recovering from his imaginary fit, he spelled over a number of the *Lancet*, dwelling long over an account of an operation of a novel kind; and ending by standing upon a chair and carefully noting the contents of the doctor's glass jars of preparations, which he turned round and round till he was tired, and came down, to finish the morning by helping himself to about a teaspoonful of chlorate of potass, which he placed in his trousers-pocket, not from any intention of taking it to purify his blood, but to drop in pinches in the kitchen fire and startle Elizabeth.

"Teach her not to say things agen my old woman," said Bob. "Just as if she can help being old!"

CHAPTER V.

A SISTER'S TRIAL.

"DON'T ask questions. There's the money; take it. You don't think I stole it, do you?"

"Stole it Hendon dear? No, of course. How can you talk so?"

"Then why don't you take it?"

"Because, as your sister, I think I have a right to know whence it comes."

"And, as your brother, seeing how we live here, in everybody's debt, I don't think you need be so jolly particular."

"However poor we are, Hendon, we need not lose our self-respect."

"Self-respect! How is a man to have self-respect, without a penny in his pocket?"

"You just showed me pounds."

"Yes, now."

"How did you come by it, Hendon?"

"Don't ask," he cried impatiently. "Take it, and pay that poor girl some wages on account, and give young Bob a tightener. Don't be so squeamish, Rich."

"I will not take the money. You deceived me once before."

"Well, if I'd told you I won it at pool you wouldn't have taken it."

"No," said Rich firmly, "I would sooner have lived on dry bread. This money, then, is part of some gambling transaction?"

"It isn't."

"Then how did you come by it?"

"Well, then, if you will have it, Poynter lent it to me!"

"Oh, Hendon, Hendon, has it come to this?" cried Richmond piteously.

"Yes, it has. What is a fellow to do? Home's wretched; one never has a shilling. The guvnor's mad over his essence, as he calls it, and I believe, if he saw us starve, he would smile and sigh."

"No, no. He is so intent upon his discovery, that he does not realize our position."

"His discovery! Bah! Lunacy! There isn't a fellow at Guy's who wouldn't laugh at me if I told him what the guvnor does. Rich, old girl, I'm sick of it! It was madness for me to go through all this training, when I might have been earning money as a porter or a clerk. Everything has been swallowed up in the fees. Why, if Jem Poynter hadn't come forward like a man, and paid the last—"

"What?"

"Well, what are you shouting at?"

"Did Mr. Poynter pay your last fees at Guy's?"

"Of course he did. Do you suppose the money was caught at the bottom of a spout after a shower?"

"Hendon, dear Hendon!"

"There, it's no use to be so squeamish. If those last hadn't been paid, it would have been like throwing away all that had been paid before."

"I did not know of this—I did not know of this!"

"Don't, don't dear! I couldn't help it. I used to feel as bad as you do; but this cursed poverty hardens a man. I fought against it; but Poynter was always after me, tempting me, standing dinners when I was as hungry as a hound; giving me wine and cigars. He has almost forced money on me lots of times; and at—at other times—when I've had a few glasses—I haven't refused it. It's all Janet's fault."

"Hendon!"

"Well, so it is!" cried the young fellow passionately. "If she hadn't thrown me over as she did—"

"To save you from additional poverty."

"No, it didn't; it made me desperate, and ready to

drink when a chap like Poynter was jolly, and forced champagne on me. I was as proud as you are once, but my pride's about all gone!"

"Hush! I will not hear you speak like that Hendon, my own darling brother! For Janet's sake—"

"She's nothing to me now. I was thrown over for some other fellow."

"How dare you, sir! You know it is not true! Dear Janet! Working daily like a slave, and offering me her hard earnings when we were so pressed."

"Did she—did she?" cried Hendon excitedly, and with his pale face flushing up.

"There," cried Richmond half-laughingly, half-scornfully, "confess, sir, that a lying spirit was on your lips. Say you believe that of Janet and that you do not still love her, if you dare!"

Hendon Chartley let his head fall into his hands, and bent down, with his shoulders heaving with the emotion he could not conceal, while his sister bent over him and laid her hand upon his head.

He started up at her touch, seized and kissed her hand, and then, going to the side of the room, he laid his arm against the panel and his brow upon it, to stand talking there.

"I can't help it, Rich dear," he groaned; "I feel like a brute beast sometimes, and as if I can never look her in the face again. I've drunk; I've gone wild in a kind of despair; and Poynter seems to have been always by me to egg me on, and get me under his thumb."

"My own brother!"

"Don't touch me, dear. I can't stop here. I'll do as Mark Heath did, and if Janet 'll wait, perhaps some day I may come back to her a better man, and she may forgive me."

There was a pause.

"I don't believe anything of her but what is good and true; God bless her for a little darling—Why, Rich!"

He turned sharply, for a low moan had escaped his sister, and he found that she had sunk into a chair, and was sobbing bitterly, with her face in her hands.

"Rich darling, I did not mean it. What have I said?"

"Nothing, nothing, dear; only you—you must not leave me."

"But Mark Heath—Ah! what a fool I am!" he cried, catching his sister in his arms. "I did not think what I was saying; and, Rich dear, hold up, I don't believe the dear old boy is dead."

"Hush, Hendon dear!" said Richmond, mastering her emotion; "I want—I want to talk to you about Mr. Poynter."

"Yes, all right. Sit down, dear, and I won't be such a fool."

"You must not leave me."

"I won't. I'll stop and fight it out like a man. And as for James Poynter, I wish I hadn't let him pay those rates."

"What?"

"I didn't like to tell you, but I let out to him about the gas and water and the rest of it, and next day he gave me all the receipts. It was one night after I'd dined with him at his club, and I was a bit primed. I thought it was very noble of him then, but when I saw it all I did nothing but curse and swear. It was nearly the death of a patient at Guy's, for I forgot what I was about. Hang it, Rich dear! don't look so white as that."

"I—I was wondering why we had not been troubled more," she stammered; and then, with her face flushing, she turned fiercely upon her brother.

"Hendon," she cried, "do you know what this means?"

There was utter silence, and Hendon Chartley turned his face away.

"I say, do you know what this means? Hendon, speak?"

"Yes."

It was slowly and unwillingly said.

"And you have encouraged this man to make advances to the woman your best friend—almost your brother—loved?"

"Oh, Rich!"

"Speak."

"No, no! I never encouraged him. I fought against it, and it has made me half mad when the great vulgar boor has sat talking about you, and drinking your health and praising you. Rich, I tell you I've felt sometimes as if I could smash the champagne bottle over his thick skull for even daring to think about you."

"And yet you have let him do all this!" cried Richmond, with her eyes flashing. "Hendon—brother, for the sake of this man's money and the comforts it would bring, do you wish to see me his wife?"

"D—n it, no! I'd sooner see you dead!" cried the young man passionately. "Say the word, old girl, and I'll fight for you as a brother should. I'll half-starve myself but what I'll get on, and pay that thick-skinned City elephant every penny I've had."

"And some day Janet shall put her arms round your neck, and tell you that you are the best and truest boy that ever lived."

"Ah! some day," said Hendon sadly.

"Yes, some day," cried Rich, clasping him in her arms. "Hendon dear, you've made me strong where I felt very, very weak, and now we can join hands and fight the enemy to the very last."

"When old Mark shall come back."

"Hush!"

"No, I'll not hush! When dear old Mark shall come back, and all these troubles be like a dream."

Richmond looked up with a sad smile in her brother's face, and kissed him once again.

"And Janet—" he said hoarsely, after he had returned her caress.

"Is acting as a true woman should. Take her as a pattern, dear, and show some self-denial."

"Why not take you, Rich?" he said kindly as he gazed in the sweet careworn face before him. "There, I won't ask you to have the money. I'm off; if I stop here longer I shall be acting like a girl. As for Poynter, if he comes and pesters you—"

"Mr. Poynter will not come," said Richmond, drawing herself up proudly. "He has acted like a coward to us both."

"One moment, Rich, said Hendon eagerly: "do you think—the governor—"

"Has taken money from him? No."

"Thank God!"

"My father, whatever his weakness, is a true gentleman at heart. He would not do this thing."

Hendon advanced a step to take his sister in his arms, but in his eyes then she wore so much the aspect of an indignant queen that he raised her thin white hand to his lips instead, and hurried from the house.

CHAPTER VI.

THE SURGERY IMP.

Dr. Chartley sat in his consulting-room, with a glass jar, retort, receiver, and spirit-lamp before him. The lamp was on the table, and made with its shaded light and that of the fire a pleasant glow, which took off some of the desolation of the bare consulting-room on that bitter night.

He had been busy over his discovery, and confessed that it was not so far advanced as he could wish.

"There is a something wanting," he had muttered more than once; and, wearied at last, he was thinking more seriously than usual of his son, of Richmond, and of James Poynter.

"It would place her above the reach of want," he said dreamily; "she would be happy if anything befell me. Yes, money is a power, and we are now so poor, so poor, that life seems to have become one bitter struggle, in which I am too weak to engage."

He sighed, and rose, walked into the miserably cold surgery, where Bob was diligently polishing the front of the nest of drawers containing drugs, and leaving threads of cotton from the ragged duster hanging upon the broken knobs.

"Good boy—good industrious boy," said the doctor, patting his head gently, before taking up a little graduated glass, pouring in a small quantity from a bottle at the top of the shelves, and after turning it into a medicine glass, he filled up with water and drank it.

Bob took the glass the doctor handed to him, smiling.

"Good for a weary troubled old man, boy," he said, "but it will kill you. *Don't touch—don't touch —don't touch.*"

He nodded and went back into the consulting-room, to compose himself upon the couch for his evening sleep, which he took according to custom, and from which he awoke refreshed and ready to work for hours, late into the night, at his wearisome chimerical task, with which he grew more infatuated the more his reason suggested that his work was vain.

The boy began to whistle very softly as the doctor disappeared. Then he washed and wiped the glass, and put it back in its place ready for use. After this he threw himself upon the settee, took hold of his right leg with his left hand, by the ankle, dragged it up, and held it across his body rigidly as if it were a banjo, and began to strum imaginary strings with his right hand, while in a whisper he sang a song about a yaller gal somewhere in the south, with close-shut eyes and a long wide mouth, and so on, through seven verses, with a chorus to each, all of which seemed to afford him the greatest gratification, and which he supplemented by leaping up and going round the surgery, holding out the imaginary instrument for contributions.

These were acknowledged with proper darky grimaces and grins, and seemed to be so abundant that Bob returned to the settee, and this time played the bones with a couple of pair saved from a brisket of beef, but without making a sound.

Another collection and another silent solo, this time on the tambourine, which the boy pretended to beat with frantic energy, ending by going on tiptoe to peep through the keyhole, and satisfy himself that the doctor was in a deep sleep.

There was no doubt about that, so the boy's hour or two of indulgence, on which he regularly counted, began.

He dashed at the settee, threw it open, stooped down to take something out, but rose again, closed the lid, and listened as if afraid of being caught.

Then shaking his head, he ran to the door, which opened into the lobby and then into the street, from which place he came, helping himself along by the wall to the settee, upon which he sank, and after lying down and laying his leg out carefully, he began to play double parts, that of surgeon and patient. For, after feeling the leg and shaking his head, he said to himself, "Ah, we'll soon put that right, my man."

Jumping up, he ran to a drawer, from which he brought splints and bandages, trotted back to the settee, and with ghastly minuteness—the result of having been present at an accident, and studious readings of Dr. Chartley's books—he proceeded to set a serious compound fracture, assuring himself that he bore it like a man, and that he need not be under the least apprehension, for in such a healthy subject the joint would knit together before long, and he would be as strong as ever.

All this was in company with the business he was

carrying on of applying the splints and bandaging the broken leg; after which, by aid of the doctor's walking-sticks, he limped to the door, as there was no one to carry him, thanked himself for his kindness, and in imagination departed, leaving himself in the character of the doctor, whose walk he imitated as he drew out a large pill-box, opened it, and took a small pinch of magnesia as if it were snuff.

Another peep at the doctor through the keyhole, and a run to the door, to make sure of there being no interruption there, and then the boy's face assumed a very serious expression. He took the cloth from the little table in the corner, rolled up the hearthrug longwise, and tied it in two places with string, and then treating it as a patient, he laid it on the settee, and drew over it the table-cover.

He was not satisfied, though, and getting a square of paper, such as would be used to wrap up a bottle of medicine, he poked his finger through twice for eyes, made a slit for a mouth, and puckered the paper for a nose.

This rough mask he tied at the end of the long roll, drew the table-cover up to the face, and then came to see the patient, carried on an imaginary conversation with a colleague, and ended by going to a cupboard and getting out a long mahogany case.

Bob's reading for the past two years had not been the wholesome and unwholesome literature provided for our youth, but the contents of the doctor's little library, the *Lancet*, and the *Medical Times*. These proceedings were the offspring.

To carry out the next proceedings, Bob took off his jacket and rolled up his sleeves; informed his colleague that it was a bad case—a diseased heart—and the only hope for the patient's life was to take it out completely.

This Bob proceeded to do with goblin-like delight. He turned the table-cover half down before opening the mahogany case, which contained a set of long amputating knives; and these he tried one after the other, to satisfy himself about the edge before commencing the operation, with great gusto, cutting the string that bound the hearthrug, making an incision, and extracting the heart. Next the place was sewn up, the cover replaced, the knives put away with horrible realism, the patient's pulse felt and a little stimulus administered—the boy taking this himself—to wit, a little ammonia and water.

Next the table-cover was drawn off, the hearthrug restored to its place; and, grinning now hugely, Bob went to a drawer, and got out the doctor's tooth-drawing instruments—for the doctor belonged to the old school, and in distant times had not been above removing a decayed and aching molar from a patient's jaw.

The boy flourished the instruments about with evident enjoyment, going as far as to take a good hold of one of his teeth, but he refrained from pulling, and rubbed his half-numbed hands.

It suddenly seemed to occur to him that he had not put on his jacket, and resuming this, and proving its many buttons to be a sham, for it fastened in a feminine manner by means of a series of hooks and eyes, he made a bound to the settee, grinning with pleasure as he threw it open, dived down, and brought out a glistening white human skull, handling it with a weird kind of delight painted in his face.

He took the ghastly object, and fixed it upon a knob, one of those upon the back of the old-fashioned chair in the middle of the room, draped it round with the table-cover; and drew back to admire his handiwork.

"Oh, if our 'Lisbeth would come in now!" he said, with a chuckle, as he rubbed his hands down his sides before proceeding to the greatest bit of enjoyment he had in his lonely life at the doctor's.

From the very first the doctor's surgery and consulting-room had had a strange fascination for him, and whenever he was missing, the maid-of-all-work, who rarely showed her face out of the dim kitchen, knew that the boy would not be playing truant from his work or playing with other lads of his age, but would be found reading, dusting, or amusing himself in the surgery, smelling bottles, opening drawers, or standing on a chair, gazing at the ghastly preparations in one or other of the row of glass jars.

His pranks he managed to keep secret, arranging to enjoy them when the doctor was asleep, and he was not likely to be disturbed.

The present was his favorite feat from its reality. There was something to go at, he always said, and for the hundredth time, perhaps, after performing the operation, and restoring with the help of a little gum, he took up the doctor's tooth-key, fixed it carefully round a perfectly sound molar in the fine specimen upon whose excellences the doctor had before now lectured to students, and steadying the skull, the boy pretended to engage in a terrible struggle; then gave a quick twitch, and brought out the tooth, which he held with a smile as he struck an attitude before its silent owner.

The boy had seemed goblin-like before, but as he now stood there before the glistening relic of mortality, over which he had partly thrown the corner of the table-cloth, the scene was weird and grim in the extreme; for the one uncovered eye-socket seemed to leer at him in company with a ghastly grin, as if rejoicing at the relief the operation had afforded.

"Now yer better, ain't yer?" said Bob. "Eh? Ah, I thought you would be. He was a tight 'un. Some 'un coming."

Quick as thought, the boy snatched the skull from the back of the chair, slipped it into the long chest, closed the lid, thrust the tooth-key back into the drawer, and had thrown the cover on the table before the door at the end of the house-passage was opened, disclosing him, in spite of all his efforts, looking as if the mischief which lurked in the corners of his mouth, and flashed from his eyes, had been running to the full extent of its chain.

CHAPTER VII.

AGONY POINT.

"Is THAT all? What a fuss over a little pain!"

What many would say to a suffering friend when sound and well themselves. What Richmond Chartley was ready to say to herself as she paced the room, with one hand pressed to her face, where the agonizing pain seemed to start as a centre, and then ramify in jerks through every nerve.

Toothache, faceache, neuralgia, according to

fashion, but maddening all the same. A pain born of care and anxiety, close confinement, abstinence, the damp unchanging foggy air, and settled in the face of a heroine, to take, as it were, all the romance out of her history.

But there it was all the same, fiercely stabbing, jerking, as if some virulent little demon were holding ends of the facial nerves in a pair of pincers, and waiting till the sufferer was a little calm for a few moments before giving the nerve a savage jig.

After the tug a pause of sickening agony, and then that slow, red-hot suffering again, as if a blunt augur was being made to form a channel beneath the teeth, so that the aching pains, as of hot lead, might run round without let or hindrance.

Neuralgia, with sleepless nights; neuralgia, with Hendon Chartley's progress at the hospital; neuralgia, with the trouble about Janet; neuralgia, with James Poynter's coarse vulgar face full of effrontery always before her, flaunting his possessions, his power, and his influence, and staring with parted lips over the words which somehow he had never yet dared to utter, but which sooner or later she knew must come.

Neuralgia, with the constant dread that some day her father would indulge too deeply in the opiate she knew he took every evening ; neuralgia, with the constant carking care of the unpaid tradespeople : and, above all, that wearisome agony, mingled with the chilling heartache and those memories of the man from whom she had parted when in his ardent desire he had told her that it was for her sake he was going to leave England, to come back some day a rich man, and ask her to be his wife.

"Dead, dead, dead!" moaned Rich, as she paced

the room; "and if I, too, could only be sleeping, for it is more than I can bear!"

But as the words left her lips, she threw her head back, and pressed her long hair from her face.

"What a coward I am!" she cried, "with others looking to me for help, and shrinking from bearing a little pain!"

She hurried to the door, telling herself that there was relief in the surgery for all she suffered; but as she went along the dark passage to the door she felt that there was one only anodyne for the greater pain she bore.

As she slowly approached there was a quick scuffling noise, a dull rattle as of something falling, and the loud closing of a heavy lid; then, as she opened the door, she found Bob turning to meet her with an innocent smile upon his face, while he was uttering a low humming noise, as if he were practising the art of imitating a musical bee.

"What have you been doing, Bob?" said Rich hastily.

"Me, Miss? Doing?" said the boy wonderingly. "I ain't a-been doing nothing. 'Tain't likely, 'mong all these here dangerous thinks;" and Bob waved his hand round the surgery, as if indicating the bottles and specimen jars.

"Because you have been warned frequently, sir, not to meddle."

"Course I have, Miss, and I wouldn't do no harm."

"Is my father asleep?"

"Jist like a top, Miss. He took his drops, and he's lying on the sofy, sleeping beautiful. You can hear him breathe if you come and put your ear to the keyhole."

"No, no," said Rich hastily; but, all the same, she walked quickly to the consulting-room door, and opened it softly, to look in and see across the table, with its chemical apparatus, the light of the shaded lamp thrown upon the calm, placid, handsome face, as the doctor lay back on the couch, taking his drug-bought rest according to his nightly custom.

Rich sighed and walked right in, the door closing behind her as she crossed the room, and stood gazing down, her head bent, and hands clasped, while for the moment she forgot her nerve-pains, and the tears started to her eyes.

"Poor father!" she sighed; "always so kind and gentle in spite of all. How do I know what he may suffer beneath the mask he wears?"

She thought of the prosperity they had once enjoyed, the many patients who came, and how, in this very room, as a child, he used to play with her long curling hair, while she, with childlike delight, emptied the little wooden bowl, and counted how many guineas papa had received that morning.

She recalled, too, the carriage in which she had sat waiting, while he, the handsome young doctor, had made his calls upon rich patients; and then, like a cloud, came creeping up the memories of the gradual decline of his practice, as he had devoted himself more and more to the dream of his life—this discovery of a vital fluid which should repair the waste of all disease, and with the indulgence in his chimera came the poverty and despair.

"Poor father!" she sighed again, bending down

and kissing the broad white forehead; "there has never been anything between us but love."

She rose slowly, went to a corner where a faded old dressing-gown hung upon a chair, and this she softly laid over the sleeping man, gazed at the fire, which was burning brightly, and then stole away with the agonizing pang, forgotten for the moment, sweeping back, and seeming to drive her mad.

"I see yer a-kissing of him, Miss," said Bob, grinning, as she closed the door.

Rich turned upon him angrily; but the boy was looking dreamily towards the doctor, and rubbing his shock head of hair.

"Don't he look niste when he's asleep like that? There ain't such a good-looking gent nowhere's about here as our master."

There was so much genuine admiration in the boy's tones that the angry look gave place to one of half amusement, half pity.

"I've often wondered whether if ever I'd had a father, he'd ha' been like the doctor, Miss. Ain't yer proud on him?"

"Yes, Bob, yes," she cried, laying her hand upon the boy's shoulder, while a strange sensation of depression, as of impending trouble, came over her, making her forget everything, and hardly notice the next act of the boy.

It is hardly fair to say that Bob's hands were dirty, but they were very coarse in grain, and discolored, the nails were worn down, and the fingers were blue with chilblains where they were not red with the chaps which roughened them; and those were the hands which took hold of Rich's and held it for a few moments against the boy's cheek, while he rubbed the said cheek softly against the smooth palm, his bright eyes looking up at her as a spaniel might at its mistress. In fact, there was something dog-like and fawning in the ways of the lad, till the hand was drawn away.

"So'm I proud on him, Miss. He is a good 'un. For it's like 'evin being here. Why, I've been here two years now, and he never kicked me once."

"And used you to be kicked before you came here, Bob?" said Rich, feeling amused, in spite of herself, at the boy's estimate of true happiness.

"Kicked, Miss? Ha, ha, ha! Why, it was 'most all kicks when it warn't pots. Old woman never kicked me; but when she'd had a drop, and couldn't get no more, she was allus cross, and then she'd hit you with what come first—pewter pot, poker, anything, if you didn't get out of the way."

Rich's brow contracted, and then for the moment the pain neutralized that of the mind.

"But she didn't often hit me," said Bob, grinning. "I used to get too sharp for her; and she didn't mean no harm. Want me to do anything, Miss?"

"No, Bob, no," said Rich, turning away to the shelves, where the bottles stood as in a chemist's shop. "Poor boy! and the place is to him like heaven!" she thought.

"Want some physic, Miss?" said the boy excitedly; "which on 'em? I knows 'most all on 'em now."

"I want the belladonna," said Rich, with her face contracted once more.

"Why, that's one o' they little bottles up a-top where they're all pisons! Whatcher want that for?" said Bob suspiciously. Then, as he read her countenance, "Whatcher got—toothache?"

Rich nodded.

"Here' hold hard! you can't reach it, Miss. Let me get on a chair. Oh, I say! Let me pull it out."

The boy's eager sympathy and desire to afford relief, grotesque as it was, seemed so genuine, so grateful to the lonely girl, that she smiled at her poor coarse companion's troubled face.

"No, no, Bob," she said gently.

"Wish I could have it instead," he cried. "I do, s'elp me!"

"It will be better soon, Bob," she said, as the boy climbed up and obtained the little stoppered bottle from the top shelf.

"That's good stuff for it, Miss," said the boy. "Bottle's quite clean. I dusted all on 'em yesterday. Here, I know! let me put some on."

"You, Bob?" said Rich.

"Yes, Miss; I know. I've seen the doctor do it twiced to gals as come and wanted him to pull out their teeth, and he wouldn't. I'll show yer."

Bob ran to a drawer and took out a camel-hair pencil, and operated with it dry upon his own face.

"I'll show yer," he cried. "You begins just in front o' the ear and makes a round spot, and then yer goes on right down the cheek and along yer chin, just as if you was trying to paint whiskers. Let m do it, Miss."

Rich hesitated for a moment, and then sat down and held her face on one side, while the boy carefully painted the place with the tincture, frowning the while and balancing himself upon the tips of his toes.

"Stop a moment, Miss," cried Bob. "Then he dropped two drops out o' this here blue bottle on a bit o' glass, and finished off with it just as you does with gum when you paint a picture."

Rich watched the boy anxiously as he took down a bottle labelled "Chloroform," but smiled and submitted patiently as the painting operation was completed.

"Feel better, Miss?" said the boy.

"Not yet, Bob; but I daresay this will do it good Now put back those bottles, and don't meddle with them, mind."

"As if I didn't know, Miss! Why, I'm up to all the doctor's dodges now. There ain't a bottle on any o' them shelves I ain't smelled; and look at them things in sperrits," he continued, pointing to the various preparations standing upon one shelf, the relics of the doctor's lecturing days. "I knows 'em all by heart. I had to fill 'em with fresh sperrit once."

Rich turned and smiled at the boy as she reached the door; and then once more the young student was left alone, to go and peep through the keyhole to see if the doctor was fast asleep, and this being so, he ran to the door by the street, turned suddenly with his head on one side, raised his hands with the helpless, appealing gesture of the sick, and walked feebly to the cushioned chest, upon which he sank, with a low moan.

It was a clever piece of acting, studied from nature, and sinking back, he lay for a moment or two sufficiently long for the supposed patient to compose himself, before he assumed another part.

Leaping up, he went on tip-toe to the consulting-room again, peeped to see that all was right, and then, drawing himself up exactly as he had seen the doctor act scores of times, he slowly approached the settee, his face full of smiling interest, and sitting down in a chair beside the imaginary patient, he went through a magnificent piece of pantomine—so good that it was a pity there was no audience present to admire. For Bob had taken the doctor's glasses from the chimney-piece, put them on, and bent over the patient.

"Put out your tongue," he said. "Hum—ha! yes! a little foul."

Then he felt an imaginary pulse, his head on one side, and an imaginary watch in his hand.

"That will do," he said, returning the imaginary watch to its airy fob. "Now sit up."

Bob's ear was applied for a few moments to the phantom patient's chest.

"Breathe hard. That's it. Now more fully. Yes. Now a very long breath."

So real was the proceeding that a spectator would have filled up the void in his mind as Bob changed his position, holding his head now at the patient's back.

"Hah!" he ejaculated, as he rose. "A little congestion! Stop a moment."

He fetched a stethoscope from the chimney-piece, but instead of using it at once, proceeded to lay his hand here and there upon his imaginary patient's breast, and tap the back over and over again.

"Hah!" he ejaculated once more, as he applied his stethoscope now after a most accurate pantomimic unbuttoning of vest and opening of a shirt-front. "Yes, a little congestion!" he said again; and going back to the chimney-piece, he set the stethescope on end as if it were a little fancy candlestick, took up a morocco case, and unhooking it, extracted therefrom a tiny thermometer, whose bulb he placed beneath his patient's arm-pit, and he was just about to see to what height the sufferer's temperature had risen, when there were steps again, and the boy had hardly time to hide the little tester, when the door opened, and, with a wild, dilated look in her eyes, Rich appeared again.

"Get me a small bottle," she said hastily.

"Ain't it no better, Miss?"

"Don't talk to me!" cried Rich; "the pain is maddening. Is my father still asleep?"

"Yes, Miss; shall I wake him?"

"No, no. The bottle—the bottle!"

The boy hastily took a clean bottle from a drawer, and fitted it with a new cork from another, by which time, with the knowledge of one who had before now made up prescriptions for her father, Rich took down the chloral hydrate, and a graduated glass, pouring out a goodly quantity ready to transfer to the bottle the boy handed her, while he still retained the cork.

This done, Rich returned the chloral hydrate to the shelf, and took down another bottle labelled *quin, sulph. sol.* From this she poured out a certain quantity, and by the time the glass had shed its last drop, Bob was ready to hand another and larger bottle, which he had taken down with eager haste, as if fearing she would be first.

Rich glanced at it, saw that it was labelled *aq. dest.*, and filled up the medicine-bottle, the boy handing the cork, and then gazing sympathetically in the pain-drawn face before him.

"Hadn't you better let me take it out, Miss?" he said, but there was no smile in answer—no reply,

Rich hurrying away, while the boy listened to her footsteps.

"Ain't she got it!" he muttered, and he stood listening still, for he heard voices at the end of the passage.

"'Lisbeth," he said, and there was a knock.

The boy opened the passage door softly, and a voice said.

"I've cut you some bread and cheese; it's on the kitchen table."

"Goin' to bed, 'Lisbeth?"

There was a grunt, and the sound of departing steps, while the boy stood gazing along the passage.

"So are you?" he exclaimed, closing the door, "Ain't she got a temper! I can't help my old woman coming. 'Tain't my fault. I shouldn't turn sulky if it was hern."

Bob did not go down for a moment, but stood thinking. Then he ran out softly, and down-stairs into the dark kitchen to fetch his supper, which he preferred to eat with the fragrant odors of drugs about him, and seated upon the chest which contained the grisly relics of mortality, and against whose receptacle the boy's heels softly drummed.

The stale bread and hard Dutch cheese rapidly disappeared, the boy looking very stolid during the process of deglutition. Then his face lit up, and for a space he went through his pantomine again, seeing patients, pocketing their fees, dressing wounds, setting limbs, and, above all, prescribing a medicine which he compounded carefully, and, to give realism to the proceedings, himself took,

It was not an objectionable medicine, being composed of small portions of tartaric acid and soda, dropped into a wineglass which contained so much water, into which had been dropped a little syrup of ginger, afterwards flavored with orange or lemon.

Tiring of this at last, Bob turned to the settee, whose lid he had opened, and he had lifted out certain anatomical specimens for his farther delectation, when there was a sharp ring at the surgery bell, and an unmistakable sound in the consulting-room—a combination which made the boy leap up, and, quick as lightning, turn out the gas, which projected on its bracket just over the settee.

This done, there was a rapid click or two of bones being replaced, the sound of the closing lid in the darkness, and by the time the consulting-room door was thrown open, and a warm glow of light shone across the surgery, Bob had effected his retreat.

"Lights out?" said the doctor going back from the door, to return directly with a burning spill, when the gas once more illumined the gloomy surgery, and to this the doctor added the ruddy glow of the street lamp, as he opened the door of the little fog-filled lobby, which intervened between him and the street.

CHAPTER VIII.

THE DOCTOR'S GUEST.

As Dr. Chartley's hand was placed upon the latch the bell-handle creaked, and the wire was sawn to and fro, while the moment the door was opened a man in a soft slouch hat and pea-jacket, with an ulster thrown over his arm, laid his hand upon the doctor's breast, thrusting him back, passing in quickly, and hastily closing and fastening the door.

The doctor stood back more in surprise than alarm, as his visitor seemed to come in with a cloud of yellowish fog, which made him look indistinct and strange, an aspect heightened by his thick beard and moustache being covered with dew-like drops—the condensation of the heavy steaming breath that came from his nostrils as he panted hard, as one pants after a long run.

"May I ask—is any one ill?" exclaimed the doctor, to whom the sudden call at any hour of an excited messenger was little matter of surprise.

"In, quick!" said the visitor hoarsely; and pressing the doctor back once more, he stood listening for a few moments as if for pursuers, and then, wild-eyed and strange, he followed Dr. Chartley into the surgery, closing the door and leaning back against it breathing heavily, his eyes staring wildly round, his sun-browned face twisting, while a nervous disposition to start and run seemed to pervade him in every gesture.

The fog and smoke which came in with him added to the strangeness of his aspect as he stood there; his hair rather long, unkempt, and wet with fog; his hands gloveless, and high boots spattered with mud and soaked with half-molten snow. There was more of the brigand in his aspect than of the honest man, and yet his drawn, agitated face was well featured and not unpleasing, besides which his wandering eyes suggested fear suffered, and not a likelihood of inspiring fear; unless it should be, as the doctor surmised, that he was mad, and the pursuit he evidently feared were that of his keepers.

It formed a strange picture—the bland, smooth shining-pated doctor facing this wild excited man, standing with his back to the door, his hands outspread as if to keep it fast, and his head half turned as he listened for the sound of steps in the stillness of the winter night.

"Will you be seated?" said the doctor blandly. "Can I be of any service?"

"Hush! Can you hear anything? There! that!" cried the new-comer, in an excited whisper. "They're coming!"

"Yes; mad," said the doctor to himself. Then aloud, "The sound you hear is the dripping of the melting snow on the pavement."

"Hah! Are you sure?"

"Oh, yes. Quite sure. Sit down, my dear sir. No, not here; come to my consulting-room. There is a fire."

The coolness of a doctor in dealing with ordinary delirium or insanity is in its way as heroic as the manner in which a soldier will face fire. To most men the advent of the strange visitor would have suggested calling in help or taking instant steps for self-preservations; but armed with weapons such as would prostrate his visitor should he prove inimical, the doctor calmly led the way into his consulting-room, poked the fire, turned up the lamp a little, and pointed to a chair, watching his visitor keenly the while to satisfy himself whether his behavior was the result of fever, drink, or an unbalanced brain.

The man glared at the doctor for a moment, stepped quickly to the room-door, opened it, listened, drew back again, closed it, and slipped the bolt on the inside.

Science-armed as he was, however, the doctor displayed no sign of trepidation, but sat down, waiting till his visitor came quickly back, threw his ulster over the back of the chair set for him, sank into it with a groan, dropped his face into his hands, and burst into a hysterical fit of sobbing.

"Hah!" said the doctor, rising, and laying his hand upon the young man's shoulder. "You seem overwrought, and—"

The stranger started back at the touch, and was about to spring up, a cry of fear escaping his lips; and his slouched hat fell off, showing his wet brow, with the tangled hair clinging to it in a matted mass.

"I thought—" he gasped. "Ah, doctor, it is you!"

"Yes, sir; sit down and let's see. You seem quite exhausted."

"Don't you know me, doctor?"

"Know you? Good heavens!" cried the doctor in astonishment. "Mark Heath?"

"Mark Heath," said the visitor, sinking back with a groan.

"We thought you must be dead," said the doctor.

"You thought I must be dead," said the young man, passing his hand over his brow, and speaking in a strange and labored way. "Yes, and I thought I must be dead—a dozen times over. I'm half dead now. What's that?"

He almost yelled the last words as he started to his feet again, his eyes wild, his right hand clinched, and his left thrust into the breast, as if in search of a weapon.

"I heard nothing," said the doctor. "Sit down."

"Some one in the street trying to get in."

"No, no, no. Sit down, my dear boy. Come, come: what's the matter?"

"Are you sure you cannot hear any one?"

"Quite, and even if I could, no one could get in without I opened the door."

"Hah!" ejaculated the young man, sinking down; brandy! for God's sake, brandy!"

The doctor looked at him, hesitated, and ended by laying his hand upon his visitor's pulse, as he sat gazing strangely at the door.

If the doctor's soft touch had been that of white-hot iron the effect could not have been greater, for with a smothered shriek the young man sprang from his chair and stood at bay by the door.

"Why, Mark Heath, my good fellow, this will not do," said the doctor blandly. "There, there, come and sit down. I was only feeling your pulse."

A faint smile came over the young man's face, and he walked back to his chair.

"I thought it was one of those fiends," he said, with a shudder.

The doctor coupled the admission with the mention of the brandy, but he was not satisfied as to the symptoms, though, seeing his visitor's exhaustion, he went to his closet and took out a spirit decanter, with tumblers, poured a little into one glass, and was about to add water to it from the little bright kettle singing on the hob, when the young man snatched at the glass, and tossed off the brandy at a gulp; but even as he was in the act of setting down the glass, he started and stared wildly round towards the door.

"Hist!" he whispered.

"Pooh! there is nothing, my dear sir," said the doctor: "why, any one would think you were being hunted by the police."

"Hunted? Yes." cried the young man thrusting the glass from him, and leaning across and seizing the doctor's wrist, "hunted—always hunted, but there were no police, doctor; why were they not near to protect me?"

"Ah, yes," said the doctor, to humor his patient, as with keen interest he watched every change in his mien. "They are generally absent when wanted. So you have been hunted, eh?"

"Hunted! Yes; like some miserable hare by the hounds. They are on my scent now. Night and day, doctor, night and day, till they have nearly driven me mad."

"Mad? Nonsense! Your brain is as sound as mine."

"Yes, now; but they will drive me mad. Night and day, I tell you—night and day, I have not dared to sleep," continued the young man wildly; "no, I have not dared to sleep, for fear that I should not wake again."

"Indeed, Heath! And who hunted you?"

"Fiends—demons in human form. I have been so that I could not sleep for fear of them. They have always been on my track—on the road through the desert, across the mountains, at the port, on shipboard; they appeared again here in England, at the docks, at the hotel, in the streets; hunted, I tell you, till I have seemed to be hunted to death."

"Be calm, my dear boy, be calm. Come, you must have sleep."

"Sleep? Yes, if I could only sleep; but no, I could not—I could not—only drink, doctor, drink; and it has never made me drunk, only keep me up —help me to escape from the devils."

"Ah, you have drunk a good deal, then?"

"Yes; brandy—brandy. It has been my only friend and support, doctor. I dared not go to an hotel; I was afraid to trust a bank; I had no friend to whom I could go; and I swore I would trust myself till I could get here safe in England."

"Where you are safe now."

"No, not yet, for they are tracking me. I got to Liverpool yesterday, and tried to throw them off; but they followed me to the hotel, and I dared trust to one there. They might have said I was mad, and claimed me; said I was a thief—a dozen things to get me into their hands."

"Be calm, Heath, be calm."

"Calm? How can a hunted man be calm with the jaws—the wet, hungry jaws—of the hounds on his heels—while he feels that in a moment they may spring upon him and rend him? Oh, doctor, doctor, you never were a hunted man."

"No, no," said the doctor blandly; "but we must master ourselves when we feel that excitement is leading us astray."

"Ay, and I have mastered myself till I can do no more," cried the young man wildly; "I escaped from Liverpool."

"Escaped?"

"Yes, and managed to get to the train, as I thought, unseen; but at the first stopping station I saw the demons pass my carriage and look in. They had changed their dress, and disguised themselves, but I knew them at once, and that my attempts were vain. It was growing dark when we reached London, and when they took the tickets I waited till the train went on again, and then leaped for my life."

"You leaped from the train?"

"Yes. I wonder I did not when it was at full speed, far away in the country."

"Hah!' ejaculated the doctor.

"I leaped from the train; but they were watching me, and they followed down the embankment and into a maze of little streets in North London yonder, where the fog and snow bewildered me; but I kept on all the evening, fearing to ask help of the police, dreading to go to an hotel for dinner. The dread, the want of sleep, have made me nearly mad. I did not know where to go, and at last, after struggling wildly to escape, I knew that my brain was going, that before long the dogs would drag me down. Then in my despair I thought of you."

"And came here?"

"Yes, for sanctuary, doctor. Save me from these devils—save me from myself. Doctor, is this to be the end of it all? I am alone—helpless: they may be listening even now. Doctor, for God's sake save me; I can do no more!"

Trembling in every limb, wildly excited, and with his despair written in every lineament of his face, Mark Heath dropped from his chair, and crept upon his knees before the doctor, holding up his clasped hands, and evidently so completely exhausted that he might have been mastered by a child.

"Yes, yes; of course, of course I will," said the doctor kindly. "There, come and lie down here on this couch."

"Lie down?" said the young man, with a suspicious look.

"To be sure; it will rest you. You are quite safe here."

"Safe? Am I safe?"

"Of course," said the doctor, spreading the fallen ulster over the young man's shivering form, as he slowly lay down.

"Stop! where are you going?"

"Only into the next room—the surgery," said the doctor, turning to face his visitor's fierce eyes as he started up from the couch.

"What for? Is it to admit those devils."

Mark Heath, in a fit of impotent rage, made a dash to reach the fireplace, but his feet were hampered by the ulster, and he would have fallen heavily had not the doctor caught him in his arms.

"Why, man," he said, "I was going to get you something to take—something to calm you. It is impossible for you to go on like this."

The young man looked at him wildly.

"I can't help it," he said, calming down. "I have been hunted till I am afraid of everybody. Save me, doctor, for you can."

"Lie down, then; there: that's better."

"Yes. I am so helpless and so weak," the poor fellow moaned. "The brandy kept me up, but it makes me wild."

"Then you shall have something that will calm you, and not make you wild," said the doctor; and he went out of the room, leaving his visitor lying down with his eyes closed.

But the moment he was alone, Mark Heath started up on one arm, listening, and thrust his hand into his breast. He was listening for the unlocking of a door; but he heard the chink of a glass and the faint gurgle of some fluid, and he sank back with a sigh of relief.

"Rich—my darling," he said softly; "it is for you, sweet—for you!"

"There," said the doctor, reëntering with a glass; "drink that, and you must have some sleep. We shall soon get you right."

"Heaven bless you, doctor!" cried the young man, hysterically pressing his hand after draining the glass. "I feel in sanctuary here. Ah," he sighed, as he sank back, "to be at rest once more, and safe! Doctor, you must guard over me and what I have here."

"Oh, yes," said the doctor, sitting down after replenishing the fire. "Did you have a rough passage back?"

"I don't know—I know nothing but that those fiends were after me to get it, and I knew that they would kill me if they could only get a chance. A hunted hare sees nothing but the hounds."

"No, of course not," said the doctor, speaking softly to keep his patient's attention, but watching him intently the while, to see the effect of his medicine. "Let's see, you have been away four years."

"Yes, four years," said Mark, speaking more calmly now. "Lost every penny, farming, doctor. No good."

"I am sorry to hear that."

"Then I tried—wagon-driving, and made a respectable living—doing regular carter's work till I had a team and wagon of my own; but I went one bad time—right across the desert, and found myself at last—seated on the last bullock of my team of twenty—by the wreck of my wagon—doctor dying—for want of water."

"Ah! that was bad."

"Yes, but I was picked up by a party who came in the nick of time. They were going by a cross journey to the diamond fields."

"Ah! you went there?"

"Yes, I went there," said the young man drowsily, and speaking in a restful manner and with many pauses. "Rough life, and for six months—no good. Then luck turned. I went on. At last found—self rich man. Rather absurd, doctor—handful of stones—stones, crystals—handful in a leather bag. Soon nothing. I often laughed. Seemed so much trash, but the right thing. Very large some of them, and I worked on—digging—and picking. Knew I was a wealthy man."

"You were very fortunate, then?"

"Yes," was the drowsy reply. "Then began the curse of it. Couldn't keep it—secret. Found out that it was dangerous. Ought to have banked, but they were—were so hard to get. 'Fraid of everybody. Felt—felt should be murdered. Nearly drove—drove me wild. Made secret—secret plans—escape—get home—old England. To bring—to bring—bag of diamonds—leather bag—worth a deal—bring home myself. Followed—followed me. Three men—part of gang out there—gamble and cheat men—at play. Always—always—on my track—hunted—at bay—sea—always watching—like tigers—Ah!"

He sprang up from his drowsy muttering state, in which he had been incoherently piercing together his imaginary or real adventures, and gazed wildly round.

"Who's that?"

"It is only I—Doctor Chartley. Lie down again."

"I thought they'd come, and I—I was telling them,

Bag of diamonds. No. Nonsense! All rubbish! Poor man. Going home. 'Nough to pay his passage. All nonsense. No diamonds; no nothing."

He had sunk back once more, and went on muttering as he dropped asleep.

The doctor sat watching him, and then rose and tapped the fire together, picking up a few fresh pieces of coal to augment the blaze, which seemed to send some of the fog out of the room.

"Wild dissipation—gambling with Nature for treasure," said the doctor softly. "Imagination. Poor wretch!"

The doctor bent down over his patient, who was now sleeping deeply, but had tossed the ulster aside, so that it was gliding down.

"Curious, this wild delirium," said the doctor, rearranging the improvised cover. "I often wonder that I have not made it a study and — Good heavens!"

He started back from the couch, and stood staring at his patient for a few minutes before advancing again, and laying his hand upon his breast gently, and then thrusting it beneath the fold of the thick pea-jacket.

"It is not delirium; they—"

The doctor hesitated a few moments after drawing back from the couch once more. Then, with his whole manner changed, he thrust his hand into the sleeping man's breast, glanced round, and, satisfied that he was not overlooked, drew forth a good-sized washleather bag, simply tied round the neck with a strip of the same skin.

"Stones," muttered the doctor, with his face agitated and his eyes glittering; and after balancing the bag in his hand and glancing at the sleeping man, he placed it upon the table, where the light of the lamp was upon it full.

Then ensued a period of hesitation, the doctor's fingers worked as he stood gazing down at the little yellowish-drab bag, and anon at his patient.

Then the newly awakened curiosity prevailed, and, unable to contain himself, he rapidly untied the string, drew open the bag, and saw that it was nearly full of large rough crystals, which sparkled in a feeble way in the light.

"Why, they must be worth a large sum," muttered the doctor, pouring out some of the stones into his hand, but pouring them back with a shudder. "How horrible!"

He did not say what was horrible, but hastily retied the bag and placed it back in the sleeping man's breast, before hurrying out into the surgery, and pacing to and fro in an agitated way.

CHAPTER IX.

THE STRANGE ACCIDENT.

A CHANGE seemed to have come over Doctor Chartley. A short time before he was calm and placid, his movements were slow, and a pleasant stereotyped professional smile made his handsome face beam. But now all was changed; the smile had gone, and, as he had passed to and fro, the light from the gas bracket displayed a countenance puckered with curious lines and frowns, while the variations of shadow caused by his constantly-changing position seemed to have altered him into another man.

He went back into the consulting-room, and looked at his patient, to find him breathing more easily and plunged into a deep sleep; and as he bent over him his hand stole toward the prostrate man's breast.

He snatched it away angrily, and returned to the surgery, to resume his hurried walk, muttering to himself, his thoughts finding utterance in sound, till he started and looked about him, as if in dread of being overheard.

Stealing back to the consulting-room, he went to the closet, and took out the bottle which contained the result of his studies, and looked at it with a sigh. Then he raised the retort and its stand from the shelf, shook his head, and replaced it.

"And if I only had money," he thought, "I could carry out my experiments at my ease, and succeed. This miserable poverty would be no more; my children would be happy; and I should win a name which would become immortal."

He shook his head, his brow grew darker, and a terrible temptation attacked him.

"No one saw him come here. It is his fancy that he has been followed. One life. What is one life in this vast world? One life. Why, my discovery perfected would be the saving of the lives of thousands, hundreds of thousands, of generations of human beings in this teeming earth. Suppose he slept and waked no more? Ah!"

The doctor stood gazing down at the sleeping man.

"Such temptations come to all," he said softly; "and I have seen so many die that the passing away of one—well, what is it but the deep long sleep into which I could make him glide without pain?

"Ah, and afterwards? Poor lad! He came to me for sanctuary, and I had betrayed my trust. How could I look in the face of my son again—in the eyes of my girl? Those clear eyes would read my secret, and I should be as one accurst."

He bent down over the sleeping man again, and in spite of himself his hand stole gently towards his heart, trembling.

"They are worth thousands," he said, "and they lie there as if of the value of a few pence. He came to me for refuge. Well, he shall not find that I have failed."

There was no tremor in his hand now as he rearranged the cover over Mark Heath's breast, to stand afterwards calmly watching his guest; and then to go out into the surgery, turn down the gas, and slowly pace the floor, thinking deeply.

Every inch of the surgery was so familiar that the darkness was the same to him as the light, and the bitter coldness of the place seemed to refresh him.

At the end of a few minutes he stood perfectly still, thinking; and then going to one of the shelves, he ran his hand softly along the top row of small bottles, took one, and turned down the gas.

As he entered the consulting-room again, he glanced at the label, nodded his head in a satisfied manner, and after a glance at his patient he seemed to make up his mind what to do.

"Perhaps I shall sleep," he thought, "and if I do he may wake. It will be a simple way."

He smiled as he took the glass into which he had previously poured the brandy, and poured in a little more, to which he added sugar, and half filled the glass with hot water from the kettle.

"He will be sure to drink that," he said, as he replaced the glass within easy reach of the sofa; and then removing the stopper from the blue bottle he held, replaced it partly in the neck, rested it upon the edge of the steaming glass, and began to count the drops which fell.

One—two—three.

Each drop at an interval after the one which had preceded it, while with his left hand he steadied the tumbler.

As the third drop fell into the glass there was a strange noise outside—a dull scuffling of feet, mutterings of voices, and then a low imperious tapping on the panel of the door.

At the first sound the doctor turned his head sharply and gazed in the direction of the door, while the rest of his body seemed to have become fixed in a cataleptic state, save that his eyes dilated and his jaw dropped.

And meanwhile, slowly and steadily, drip—drip—drip—drip, the globules of fluid fell from the tip of the blue bottle into the steaming glass at last in quite a stream.

A strange dread had overcome the doctor. His patient's words about his diamonds had proved to be true; were the rest, then, true—that he had been pursued by men whose aim it was to plunder, perhaps murder him, and they had really traced him down here?

"Bah! am I turning childish?" said the doctor, starting up, and letting the stopper fall back into its place in the bottle, just as his patient moaned slightly, turned impatiently in his sleep, and the water glided to the floor."

The doctor stooped quickly, raised it, and threw it over his patient, and, as he bent over him, listened intently to the repetition of the tapping.

"It might be," he said softly. "Pish! absurd! The wanderings of a diseased mind."

Catching up the bottle from where he had placed it on the table, he walked quickly towards the door, paused, returned, and stooped as if to pick up the poker. Then smiled at his folly.

He passed softly out of the door, and closed it after him, to go to the shelves in the dark, where he made a clicking noise among the bottles, as he reached up; for there in the darkness the feeling once more assailed him that his patient might be right, while for the third time, more plainly heard now, there came a sharp tapping.

The doctor crossed to the gas bracket, turned it up, and as its light filled the surgery, he walked boldly to the lobby door, opened it, and the dull red glare from the fanlight over the outer door shone upon his handsome placid face.

The next moment he had opened the outer door, and was gazing at a group of three men.

Mark Heath's announcement flashed through his brain once more, and then gave place to the ideas furnished by his visitors.

"Thought you were a-bed. Couldn't find the bell. This cursed fog, sir. Our friend here knocked down by a cab, and we saw your red light as we were trying to get him to our hotel."

"Tut, tut, tut!" ejaculated the doctor. "Bring him in, gentlemen."

He glanced at his visitors. Saw that they were well-dressed men in ulsters and low-crowned hats, and that the speaker was a well-built fellow with a closely-cut beard; while another was a rather Mephistophelean-looking man, with cheeks closely shaven, and upper lip bearing a bristly moustache.

Between them they supported a slight, young-looking companion, who was moaning slightly, but evidently making an effort to be firm.

"Mind, Harry—Rogers," he said, in a high-pitched voice, "it's as if something red hot was running through my chest! Ah-h-h!"

"Support him, gentlemen," said the doctor. "Mind he doesn't faint. Here, quick! Here!"

He spoke in sharp, decided tones, as he directed and helped them to lay the injured man upon the settee, where he subsided with a querulous cry, grinding his teeth the while, and compressing his lips.

"Kindly shut both doors," said the doctor; and the man who had first spoken, and who looked very pale, obeyed.

"So cursedly unlucky!" he said excitedly. "I never saw such a fog. They've no business to allow men to drive fast on a night like this."

"Don't talk, old chap. Not serious, I hope, doctor?" said the Mephistophelean man. "Cab seemed to come out of the fog, and he was knocked down. I got an ugly blow on the shoulder."

"Get me some brandy," said the injured man faintly. "My chest's crushed."

"No, no, not so bad as that," said the doctor kindly. "You shall have a stimulus soon. Now, then, suppose we see what the damage is. A broken rib, I expect, and that will only mean a little pain. Now, then."

His busy fingers were rapidly and tenderly unbuttoning the injured man's coat, while a gasping moan came from his lips.

"Hurts me horribly—to breathe, doctor."

There was a gasping sound, and the Mephistophelean man reeled, tried to save himself, and fell against the consulting-room door, which somehow flew open, revealing the sleeping figure of Mark Heath on the couch.

"My dear sir—faint?"

"I beg your pardon," doctor, said the sinister-looking man. "Sick as a great girl. I can bear pain, but to see him like that turned me over. No, no, see to him; I'm better now."

The doctor continued his task, while the door swung to once more.

"Still feel faint?" said the doctor, without looking up.

"Oh, no; it's all gone now. I really am ashamed."

"Nothing to be ashamed of, my dear sir. It is a man's nature. Now I shall be obliged to ask one of you to lend me a little assistance here."

The bearded man stood eady, and exchanged a glance with his Mephistophelean companion, who was behind the doctor now.

"Ah!"

Dr. Chartley uttered a quick ejaculation, for, as he bent over his patient, the man behind struck him a heavy blow with a short thick life-preserver, and, quick almost as lightning, delivered another crashing stroke on the back of the head.

Without so much as a groan, merely a catching at the air, the doctor fell forward upon his supposed patient, and then rolled with a dull heavy sound upon the carpet, to lie motionless—to all appearance dead.

"Yah! what a butcher you are, Rogers!" said the sham patient, in a querulous high-pitched tone.

"Hold your row! Quick! Listen at that door."

The sham patient sprang to the door at the end of the passage, opened it softly, and stood listening.

"All right," he whispered, "still as death."

"Curse you! hold your row about death," whispered the other as the door was closed. "Lock it."

"I was going to," said the younger man, turning the key softly. "Is he there, Harry?"

"Yes; all right," came in a whisper from the bearded man, who had softly opened the consulting-room door and peered in at the sleeping figure upon the couch. "Quick! come on."

The man addressed as Rogers had stooped down and then gone on one knee, thrusting the life-preserver into his pocket while he examined the doctor, and not noticing that it slipped out on to the skirt of his coat, and rolled aside as he finished his examination, and satisfied himself that there was nothing to be apprehended there.

He started up, and followed his companion on tiptoe, and the next minute they were gazing down at the man they had tracked from the diamond-fields and run to earth at last.

"Hah!" exclaimed the Mephistopheles of the party; "that's right. Give him one if he moves."

This to his bearded companion, who had drawn a life-preserver similar to that his companion had used, as he bent over the sleeping man.

"He has had a dose," was whispered back. "You can smell his breath."

"Brandy. All right!" cried the youngest of the three, catching up the decanter, smelling it, tasting it with a loud smack of the lips, and pouring out a goodly portion in the empty glass, he handed it to his first companion. "Here, Harry."

"Sure it's all right?" was whispered back.

"Swear it. Now, Rogers."

"Here's mine," said the man, with a grin. "Hot with. Quick, lads!"

"Don't touch that," was on the younger man's lips; but his companion raised the glass with a laugh, and as he followed his example by putting the decanter to his mouth, the doctor's assailant literally poured the contents of the tumbler down his throat, and then stood still, put the glass back on the table, gasping and staring straight before him.

His companions were not heeding him, for each drank eagerly of the brandy, and were setting down the decanter and glass, when the younger man spoke:

"Why, Rogers, old chap!"

The man addressed turned his wild staring eyes at him for a moment, as if to answer, and then walked blindly between the sofa and the table, as if to go straight to the wall, reeled and fell, catching at the cloth, which he dragged aside, nearly causing the lamp to go crashing on the floor.

For a few moments the others stood aghast, staring at their prostrate companion, who writhed slightly for a brief period, uttering a curious sound, and then lay upon his back, stretched out motionless.

The younger man was the first to recover himself.

"Help!" he gasped, in a hoarse whisper.

"Hush!" cried his companion; "are you mad?"

He raised his life-preserver threateningly, and the

other gazed at him with ghastly face and staring eyes.

"What shall we do?" he whispered.

"Keep your head, and don't be a fool," was the reply.

As the bearded man spoke he went down on one knee, thrust his hand into his comrade's breast, and then rose quickly.

"What is it, Harry—poison?"

"Yes, grim death, lad."

"Then, we've got it, too."

"No—all right. The fool! Smell that glass."

He took up and held the tumbler to his nose, and then passed it to his companion, who smelt it, and put it down with a shudder.

"Come on," he panted; "let's get away."

"Without the diamonds—now?"

"I'm no use," groaned the younger man.

"Hold up, curse you! It's fortune of war. One man down. Prize-money to divide between two instead of three."

"Hah!" ejaculated the other, upon whom his comrade's words acted like magic. "I'm all right, now. Quick! let's have 'em!"

The elder man had already thrust his hand into Mark's breast.

"Well?"

"All right."

"Are they there?"

"Yes; safe enough."

"Get 'em out, then, and let's go. Curse it! Look at old Rogers' eyes."

There was a dull heavy sound of a door banged, and the two men started up in an agony of dread that the spoil for which they had toiled so patiently had long, never getting it within their clutch till now, was about to be snatched away.

It was a door that had been banged, and in their ignorance of the configuration of the place they did not realize that it was in the next house.

"Keep your head," said the elder man.

"Right. I'm cool enough," was the reply. "Quick! get 'em out, and let's go!"

"It would take half an hour to get at them. He has a belt buckled round his waist under everything, and there'll be stones sewn into his clothes all over."

"Curse it all!"

"Hush! Quick! Take hold of that ulster, and there's his hat."

"What are you going to do?"

"We've got him. He's drugged, and we can do what we like."

"What! bring him away?"

"Yes. Quick! take hold of that arm!"

"But if he wakes?"

"Send him to sleep, as we did the doctor. Now, hold your row, do as I do, and keep your head."

The younger man obeyed, and catching Mark Heath's arm, as his companion had done on the other side, they placed his hat upon his head, and in a half-conscious way he made an effort to walk, so that they had no difficulty in getting him into the surgery.

"Now, then, button-up. I'll hold him," said the elder man.

"But when we get him in the street?" whispered the other

"Well—what? He's drunk. We'll get him in a cab. No one will interfere. Leave it to me, and back me up. Quick! shut that door; and then turn on the light."

The orders were obeyed; and as soon as they stood in the darkness the lobby-door was opened, where the red light gave them sufficient illumination to finish their proceedings.

Another minute, and, their victim's arm well gripped on either side, the elder man said hoarsely,

"Ready?"

"Yes; but are you sure that he had the stuff on him?"

"Trust me for that. Now, be cool, and the diamonds are ours. Off!"

The outer door was opened, and with very little difficulty Mark Heath was half-lifted, half-led outside, in an inert, helpless condition, his brain steeped in sleep, and his mind a blank. Then the two men stood in the snow, listening for a sound within the house.

It was the elder who spoke then:

"Get your arm well under him. Hold hard! Shut the door. Mind he don't slip down. It's dark as pitch. Now, then, come on."

At that moment John Whyley turned on his lamp.

CHAPTER X.

"AY, MARRY IS'T; CROWNER'S QUEST LAW."

A JURY of men, chosen with the careful selection always made by the coroner's officer, and with such extraordinary happy results, sat solemnly and listened to the evidence, after hearing the coroner's preliminary address, and viewing the body of the deceased.

Witness by witness, all were examined. John Whyley told all he knew, and produced the life-preserver; Richmond Chartley, brought from her father's bedside, where he lay perfectly insensible, gave her account of the proceedings, and directly after joined Janet Heath, who was her companion, and sat down to try once more to disentangle her thoughts, which, from the time she had left the surgery with the bottle of chloral till she was alarmed by the persistent ringing of the doctor's night-bell, had been in a state of wild confusion.

Hendon Chartley gave his evidence. How he had been spending the evening with a gentleman of his acquaintance, and on letting himself in with his latch-key he had heard voices in the surgery, and gone there.

Mr. James Poynter, the gentleman with whom Hendon Chartley had been dining corroborated the last witness, and seemed disgusted that he had not a better part to play, especially after his announcement to the coroner that he was a great friend of the family.

For some reason of their own, the sapient jury men exchanged glances several times during the evidence of the last two witnesses, and shook their heads, while one man began to make notes on the sheet of paper before him with a very scratchy pen whereupon two more immediately caught the complaint, and the foreman regretted to himself that he wasn't as handy with ink as he could wish.

The surgeon was of course a very important witness, and he told how the man upon whose body the inquest was being held had undoubtedly died of an excessive dose of hydrocyanic acid, of which poison there was, naturally enough, a bottle in the doctor's surgery; but how it had been administered, whether by accident, purposely, or with suicidal intent, it was impossible to say; and apparently the only man who could throw any light upon the subject was Doctor Chartley himself, who was now lying in a precarious state, perfectly insensible from the pressure of bone upon the brain, and too feeble for an operation to be performed.

"Not the only man," said one of the jury; "three men were seen by the policeman to leave the surgery."

The coroner said "Exactly;" and there was a murmur of assent; while, after stating that it was impossible to say how long Dr. Chartley would be before he could appear, and that it was quite possible that he would never be able to give evidence at all, the surgeon's evidence came to an end.

Elizabeth Gundry was called; and a frightened-looking smudgy woman came forward, trembling and fighting hard not to burst into tears, hysterical sobbing having filled up so much of her time since the foggy night that her voice had degenerated into an appealing whine. She was smudgy-looking, but undoubtedly clean; only life in underground kitchens, and the ingraining of London blacks with the baking process of cookery, had given her skin an unwholesome tinge, which her reddened eyes did not improve.

Questioned, she knew nothing but that she thought she had heard the doctor's bell ring; but that she always put her head under the clothes if she did hear it, and she did so that night. Further questioned why, she said with sobs that it was a very large house, and nobody was kept but her and Bob; and she was "that tired when she went to bed that she thought it weren't fair to expect her to get up and answer the night-bell, and so she never would hear it if it rang. It warn't her place; for though she did housemaid's work, and there was two sets of front-door steps, she considered herself a cook."

Here there was a furious burst of sobbing, and the foreman of the jury wanted to know why.

Now he, being a pleasant-looking man, won upon Elizabeth Gundry more than the coroner did, that gentleman being suggestive of an extremely sharp ratting terrier grown fat. So Elizabeth informed the foreman that her grief was, of course, partly on account of master, and she thought it very shocking for there to be a murder in "our house;" but what she wanted to know was what had become of Bob, whom she was sure one of those bad men had smuggled away under his coat.

Of course, this brought Bob to the front, and, growing garrulous now, Elizabeth informed everybody that Bob was a regular limb, but evidently a favorite; and since Bob had answered her out of the surgery regarding his supper, Bob had not been seen or heard of, and it was her opinion that he had been killed, so as not to tell all he knew.

Bob's bed had not been slept in; Bob's hat was hanging in the pantry, and the police had not been able to discover where Bob had gone.

The mystery seemed to thicken, and Elizabeth was questioned till she broke down sobbing once more, after declaring that Bob was the mischievousest young imp as ever lived, but she was very fond of him; and if it haden't been for his wicked old tipsy mother, who was no better than a thief, there weren't a dearer, more lovable boy in the "old world."

The sergeant of police and John Whyley made notes, afterwards compared, about Bob and his mother, and Elizabeth went off crying and refusing to be comforted because of Bob.

Then the sergeant stated perspiringly in the hot room, buttoned up in his coat, that the cabman had been found; and in due course a red-nosed, prominent-eyed member of the four-wheeled fraternity corroborated John Whyley's evidence as to the three men whom he took in his cab. He reiterated the statement that "one on 'em was very tight;" told that he drove them to an hotel in Surrey Street, close to the Embankment, and corrected himself as to the driving, because "You see, gents, it was like this here: the fog was that thick, if you sat on the box you couldn't see the 'oss's tail, let alone his ears, and you had to lead him all the way."

Did the men go into the hotel?

He couldn't say; they helped out the one as was so very tight, and they gave him arf-suff'rin—first money he'd took that night, and the last, on account of the fog.

And where did the three men go—into the hotel?

He didn't know; they seemed to him to go into the fog. Everythink went into the fog that night or come out on it. It was all fog as you might 'most ha' cut with a knife; and when he had a wash next morning, his face was that black with the sut you might ha' took him for a sweep.

But the man who seemed to be drunk, did he say anything?

Not a word.

Would he know the men again?

Not likely; and besides, if he took notice of all parties as was very tight, and as he took home in his keb, he'd have enough to do. That there fog was so thick that—

The coroner said that would do, and after the people at the hotel had been called to prove that no one had entered their place after eleven o'clock that night, and that the bell had not been rung, the coroner said that the case would have for the present to be left in the hands of the police, who would, he hoped, elucidate what was at present one of the mysteries of our great city. He did not think he was justified in starting a theory of his own as to the causes of the dramatic scene that must have taken place in Dr. Chartley's surgery. They were met to investigate the causes of the death of this man, who was at present unknown. No doubt the police would be able to trace the three men who left the surgery that night, and during the adjournment Dr. Chartley would probably recover; and so on, and so on; a long harangue in which it seemed as if the fog, of which so much mention had been made, had got into the evidence.

Finally the coroner said that he did not think he should be doing his duty if he did not mark the feeling he had with respect to the conduct of the police-constable John Whyley.

The gentleman in question glowed, for he felt that he had suddenly become a prominent personage, with chevrons upon his arm to denote his rise in rank. Then he froze, and his face assumed a terribly blank expression, for the coroner went on to say that never in the whole course of his experience, which now extended over a quarter of a century, had he been cognizant of such utterly crass stupidity as that of this policeman—a man who, in his opinion, ought to be dismissed from the force.

John Whyley wished a wicked wish after the jury had been dismissed, and orders given for the burial of the Mephistophelean-looking man, lying so stiff and ghastly in the parish shell—and John Whyley's wish was that it had been the coroner instead of Doctor Chartley who had got "that one—two on the nob."

CHAPTER XI.

MR. POYNTER POLISHES HIS HAT.

JAMES POYNTER rang four times at Dr. Chartley's door-bell, and rapped as many at the great grinning knocker tied in flannel, before he heard the chain put up and the lock shot back, to display the smudgy unwholesome countenance of Elizabeth Gundry, who always blinked like a night-bird when forced to leave her dark kitchen.

"There, hang it, woman, open the door!" cried Poynter. "Do you take me for a thief?"

"No, sir, I didn't know it was you; but I am so scared, sir, and they ain't found Bob yet."

Elizabeth did not hear what James Poynter said about Bob, for she closed the door, took down the chain, opened slowly and grudgingly, and the visitor entered.

"How's the doctor?"

"Awful, please, sir, just; he's there with his eyes shet, as if he was going to die, and Miss Rich and Miss Janet taking it in turns to sit up night and day."

"Ask Miss Chartley to come down and see me."

"Which, please, sir, she said as she couldn't see nobody now."

"You go and do as I tell you."

"Which it ain't my place, sir, to answer the front door-bell at all. Poor Bob!"

She ended with a sob, and put her apron to her eyes. "I say," said Poynter, giving her apron a twitch and dragging it down, "look here."

"Well, I'm sure!" began Elizabeth indignantly.

"Look here; have your wages been paid?"

"Lor', no, sir, not for ever so long," said Elizabeth, with an air of surprise at the absurdity of the question.

"Then look here, Elizabeth: you know what I come here for, don't you?"

"I think I can guess, sir," said the woman, suddenly becoming interested and smiling weakly.

"Of course you can. You're a sharp 'un, that's what you are. So look here: the day I'm married I'll pay your wages, and I'll give you a fi'-pun note to buy yourself a new bonnet and gown. Now go up and say I'm waiting to see Miss Richmond on particular business."

Elizabeth's eyes opened widely, and there was a peculiar look of satisfaction therein as she closed the door, led the way into the dining-room, and then, after giving the visitor a nod of intelligence, she left him to go up-stairs and deliver her message.

"Pah! how the place smells!" muttered Poynter. "Any one would think that chap was here now. A nasty, damp, fusty hole!"

He listened eagerly, but the step he hoped to hear was not coming, and he began to walk up and down, twisting his silk handkerchief round, and polishing his glossy hat the while.

"I'm screwed up now," he muttered. "I'm not afraid of her. She can't say no, but if she does, she's got to learn something. Perhaps she don't know what putting on the screw means, and I shall have to teach her. All for her good. Hah!"

There was no mistake now; a step was descending the stairs, and James Poynter once more looked round for a mirror for a final glance; but there was nothing of the kind on the blank walls, and he had to face Richmond unfurbished.

She entered the room, looking quite calm, but very pale, and the blue rings about her eyes told of her sufferings and anxiety. There was a slight heightening of her color, though, for a few moments, as the visitor advanced with extended hand, in which she placed hers for a few moments before motioning him to a seat.

"How's the doctor?" he said huskily, and then coughed to clear his throat.

"Very, very ill, Mr. Poynter," was the reply. "I am sorry, but I must ask you to please see Doctor Maurice, who has promised to attend any of my father's patients if they called."

"Oh! bother Doctor Maurice! I'm better now. Quite well."

James Poynter had partaken of the greater portion of a bottle of champagne before he came, so as to screw himself up, as he termed it; and there was plenty of decision of a rude and vulgar type as he spoke.

"I beg your pardon; I thought you had come to consult my father. You have come to see how he was?"

"No, I didn't? You know what I 've come for."

Richmond did know, and perfectly well; but as she scorned to make use of farther subterfuge, she remained silent.

"I'm a plain fellow, Miss Rich, and I know what's what," he said, "Hendon and I've had lots of chats together about money matters, and you want money now."

"Mr. Poynter!"

"Now, now, now! sit down, and don't get in a wax, my dear, with a man who has come as a friend. I'm well enough off now, but I know the time when a half-crown seemed riches, and if a friend had come to me, I'd ha' said 'Bless yer!'"

"If you have come as a friend of my brother, Mr. Poynter, I am grateful."

"Now, don't put me on one side like that, Miss Rich—don't. I have come as a friend—the best of friends. I know what things are, and that you're pushed for money."

"Mr. Poynter!" indignantly.

"Yes, I know what you are going to say. 'Tain't put delicate. Can't help that. I'm a City man of business; but if it ain't put delicately it's put honest. We don't put things delicately in the City."

"I have no doubt of your intentions, Mr. Poynter, and I am grateful."

"Thank you, and that's right. Now, don't kick

at what I'm going to say, and let it hurt your pride, because it is only between you and your best friend —the man as loves you. There, I came to say that, and I'm glad it's out."

"Mr. Poynter," said Rich hastily, "I am worn out. I am ill. I have that terrible trouble in the house. It is not the time to speak to me like this."

"That's where you're wrong, my dear; for when should your best friend come if it isn't when you're sick, and so pushed for money that you don't know where to turn?"

"Oh, the shame of it!" moaned Rich to herself, as her eyes flashed with mortification, while Poynter went on polishing his hat.

"You see I know all about it, and I want to show you that I'm no fine-weather friend."

"Mr. Poynter I have told you that I am ill; will you please to bring this visit to an end? I—I cannot bear it."

"Yes, you can," he said, in what was meant to be a soothing tone; "let's have it over at once, and have done with it. I wont hurry you. I only want to feel that it will be some day before long; and till then here's my hand, and it don't come to you empty. Say what's troubling you, and what you want to pay, and there's my check for it. I don't care how much it is."

"Mr. Poynter," cried Rich, "you force me to speak out. I cannot take your help, and what you wish is impossible."

"Oh, no, it isn't!" he said, smiling, and leaving his handkerchief hanging on his hat as he tried to take her hand, which she withdrew; "I saw the doctor the other day, before this upset. We had a long chat over it, and he was willing."

"What! my father willing?"

"To give his consent? Yes."

"It is impossible!" cried Rich.

"Oh, no, it isn't, and what's more, Hendon and I have often chatted this over together, and he's willing, too. Now, I say, what is the use of making a fuss over it? There, we understand one another, and I want to help you at once."

"Mr. Poynter," cried Rich, "I now calmly and firmly tell you that what you wish can never take place. Will you allow me to pass?"

"No," said Poynter, flushing angrily, "I won't. Now, don't put me in a temper over this by being foolish. What's the good of it? You know it's for the best, and that as my wife you can help the old man, and get your brother on. See what a practice you could buy Hendon by and by."

"Mr. Poynter, I have already told you, I can say no more."

"Don't say any more, then," he cried, barring her way of exit, as he gave his hat a final polish, and pocketed his handkerchief. "I respect you—no, I love you all the more for holding out; but there's been enough of it now, so let's talk sensibly. Come, I say. Why, after this upset some men would have fought shy of the place, even if you'd had a fortune. I don't: I come to you quite humble, and say what shall I do for you first?"

Rich stood before him pale, and with her eyes flashing in a way that penetrated even the thick hide of his vanity, and was unmistakable.

"Look here," he said angrily, "don't go on like that. It makes a fellow feel put out."

Richmond once more essayed to leave the room, but Poynter stayed her.

"Look here," he said, "I'm a City man, I am. I began life with nothing, but I said to myself I'd make my fortune, and I've made it. While other fellows were fooling about, I worked till I could afford to do as they did, and then, perhaps, I had my turn. Then I saw you, and when I had seen you I said to myself that's the woman for my wife."

"Mr. Poynter!"

"Yes, and some day it shall be Mrs. Poynter. I said it should, and so it shall!"

"Mr. Poynter, will you leave this house?"

"No, I won't," he replied bitterly, "not till you've thrown all this nonsense aside, and made friends. What a temper! Now, look here, Rich, I've been afraid of you. I've come here to see the doctor, and I've shivered when I've seen you. I've wanted to speak to you, but my tongue has seemed to stick to the roof of my mouth; but that's all over now, and we're going to understand one another before I go."

"Sir, this is insolence!"

"Insolence!" he said, with the champagne effervescing as it were, in his veins. "No, it's love."

Richmond rang the bell.

"Bah!" he said, "what of that? When the girl comes—if she does—I shall tell her to go, for I mean to be master here now."

"Coward!"

"No, not a coward now," he replied, laughing. "Rich, do you know what I can do if I like? I can come down on brother Hendon for all he owes me, and how would it be then?"

Richmond winced, and the flush in her cheeks paled away, while Poynter saw it, and went on:

"What should you say if I was to act like a business man would, and come down on your father!"

"What? My father! He does not owe you money?"

"Doesn't he!" said Poynter, with a mocking laugh. "You see you don't know everything, my dear. Come, what's it going to be—peace or war?"

"War!" said Richmond firmly. "My father cannot owe you money, and as to my brother, he would sooner die than see his sister sold as a slave to pay his debts."

"Would he?" snarled Poynter. "Why he's as weak as water; I can turn him around my thumb. You tried to keep him away. He wouldn't own it; but I know. He came, though, all the same, when I asked him; and he will come, too, as often as I like, and he'll help me to make you— Bah! nonsense! Come, don't let's talk like this: you're out of sorts, and no wonder, and I've come at a bad time. To-morrow you'll be cool, and you'll put that little hand in mine, and say, 'James Poynter, you've acted like a man and my best friend, and I won't say no.'"

He tried to take her hand, but she shrank from him.

"Sir, I beg that you will not come here again," she said, drawing herself up. "I am not blind to your position with my brother, but—"

"Your brother's a weak-minded young fool!" cried Poynter, who had now thoroughly become roused, so withering was the contempt written in Rich's eyes; "and—"

He stopped short, for in the heat of the encounter neither had heard the latch-key in the front door, nor the opening of that of the room, to admit Hendon Chartley, who stood still for a few moments, and then strode to his sister's side and put his arm round her.

"Yes," he said hoarsely, "I have been a weak young fool, James Poynter, to let you play with me as you pleased; but please God, with my sister's help, I'm going to be strong now, and if you don't leave this house I'll kick you out."

"You kick me out! snarled Poynter, snatching his handkerchief from his pocket and polishing his hat savagely; "not you! So it's going to be war, is it? Why, if I liked— There, you needn't threaten. I'm not going to quarrel with you, my lad, because we're going to be brothers."

"Brothers!" cried Hendon, in tones of contempt.

"Yes, my lad, brothers. I've gone the right way to work, and you know it, too. There, we're all peppery now. Rich, my dear, you know what I've said. I'm not angry. It was only a flash, and you won't like me any the worse for speaking out like a man. Next time I come we shall be better friends."

He gave his hat a final polish, flourished his handkerchief, and left the room.

"Hendon, Hendon, what have you done?" cried Richmond, as soon as they were alone. "Had we not trouble enough without this?"

"The cad!" cried Hendon angrily.

"And after what had passed you went to him again!"

"How could I help it?" said the young man, with a groan. "I owe him money, and it's like a chain about my neck. He tugs it, and I'm obliged to go."

"And he hinted that our poor father was in his debt."

"The governor? Oh, Rich!"

Richmond said nothing, but returned to her watching by her father's pillow, asking herself whether the chain was being fitted to her own limbs, and whether, to save those she loved, she was to become this man's slave.

CHAPTER XII.

THE DREAMS OF A FEVER.

A DREAMY sensation of cold and thick darkness and stumbling on and on, with a dull light glowing about his head and fading away directly, then more darkness and stumbling on, and once more a dull yellow glow, and this fading away, with the darkness increasing. Then a slight struggle, and a few petulant remonstrances.

Why wouldn't the doctor let him sleep?

Then another feeble struggle, a sensation of passing through the air, a sudden plunge into the icy water, and then utter darkness, and a noise, as if of thunder, in his ears.

But the sudden immersion was electric in its effect, sending a thrill through nerve and muscle, though the brain remained still drowsily inert, while the natural instinct of desire for life chased away the helpless state of collapse; and Mark Heath, old athlete, expert swimmer, man hardened by his life in the southern colony, rose to the surface, and struck out, swimming slowly and mechanically, as if it were the natural action of his muscles.

On and on, breasting the icy water, keeping just afloat, but progressing blindly where the tide willed; on and on through the darkness, with the yellow fog hanging like a solid bank a few feet above his head, as if the rushing of the water were cutting the lower stratum away.

Now a yellow light shone weirdly through the mist, came into sight, and after glowing for a moment on the murky current, died away.

On still, as if it were the tide—that last tide which sweeps away the parting spirit—stroke after stroke, given mechanically; and then there was another light—a dull red light, then an angry glow—a stain as of blood upon the black water; and it, too, died away, but not till it had bathed the upturned face with its crimson hue.

Onward still, the icy water thrilling the swimmer through and through, but seeming to bring with it no dread, no sense of horror, no recollection of the past, no fear of what was to come: the sensation was that he was swimming as one swims without effort in a dream.

A blow from some dark slimy object along whose side he glided, and then on once more.

Another blow against something which checked him for a time, and turned him face downward, so that the thundering recommenced in his ears; there was the sense of strangulation; and then he was steadily swimming on once more, past moored barge with its lights, past steamboat pontoon; and then with a rush he was driven against a stone pier; his hands grasped at the slimy stones without avail, he was turned in an eddy around and around, sucked under, and rose again, to swim on and on, till at last, in the darkness, his hands touched the muddy pebbles of the river shore, his knees struck heavily, and he crawled through a pool, and then staggered to his feet, with the water streaming from him.

What next? It was all as in a dream, in which, in the gloom of the thick night, he stumbled upon a flight of slippery steps, and walked up and up, and then along a road which he crossed again and again, and always walking on and on.

At times he guided himself by mechanically touching a cold rough stony wall, till somehow it was different and felt slippery, and his hand glided over the side.

Then darkness, and a sense of wandering. How long? Where? Why was he wandering on?

It was all a dream, but changed to a time when his head was as it were on fire, and he was climbing mountains where diamonds glistened at the top, but which he could not reach, though he was ever climbing, with the sun burning into his brain, and the diamonds that he must find farther and farther away.

And so on, and so on, in one long weary journey, to reach that which he could not attain, and at last oblivion—soft, sweet, restful oblivion—with nothing wrong, nothing a trouble, no weariness or care: it was rest, sweet rest, after that toilsome climb.

The next sensation was of a cool soft hand upon his brow, and Mark Heath opened his eyes, to gaze into those of a pale, grave-looking woman in white, curiously-shaped cap; and she smiled at the look of intelligence in his face as he said softly.

"Who are you?"

"Your nurse," was the reply.

"Nurse?"

One word only, but a chapter in its inquiring tone.

"Yes," she said gently; "you have been ill. Don't try to talk. Take this, and lie quite still."

Another long, dreamy time, during which there were noises about his head—the gentle, pleasant voice of his nurse, and the firm, decisive voice of the doctor. It might have been hours, it might have been days or weeks, he did not know; and then came the morning when he seemed to awaken from a long disturbed sleep, full of terrible dreams, with a full realization of his position.

He looked about him, and there were people in beds on either side, while a row of windows started from opposite to him, and went on right and left.

At last he saw the face of the woman whom he felt that he had seen leaning over him in his dream.

She came to his bedside.

"Well?" she said, with a pleasant smile.

"Is this a hospital?" he said eagerly.

"Yes."

"And I have met with some accident—hurt?"

"No," was the reply; "not an accident. You have been ill."

"Ill? How came I here?"

He looked wildly in the calm soft face before him, and behind it there seemed to be a dense mental mist which he could not penetrate. There was the nurse; and as he lay, it seemed to him that he could think as far as her presence there, and no further.

"You had better wait till the doctor has been round."

"If you don't tell me what all this means," he said impetuously, "you will make me worse."

She laid her hand upon his forehead, to find that it was perfectly cool, and he caught her fingers in his as she was drawing them away.

"Don't keep me in suspense," he said piteously.

"Well, I will tell you. The police brought you here a fortnight ago. They found you lying in a doorway, drenched with water and fast asleep. You were quite delirious, and you have been very ill."

"Ill? Yes, I feel so weak," he muttered, as he struggled to penetrate the mist which seemed to shut him in, till the nurse's next words gave him a clue to the way out.

"We do not even know who you are; only that they suppose you to be a sailor who has just left his ship."

"Heath—Mark Heath," he said quickly.

"Ah! And your friends? We want to communicate with them."

"My friends! No; it would frighten her, poor little girl!"

"The cause for alarm is passed," said the nurse gravely.

"Yes. Ah! I begin to recollect now," he said. "Send to Miss Heath—my sister—19 Upper Brunswick Avenue, Bloomsbury."

"Yes; and now lie still."

The nurse left him, and he lay thinking, and gradually finding in the mist the pieces of the puzzle of his past adventure, till he seemed to have them nearly all there.

Then came the doctor with a few words of encouragement.

"You'll do now," he said. "Narrow escape of losing your hair, young fellow. Next time you come from sea don't touch the drink."

Mark Heath lay back thinking, and with the puzzle pretty well fitted together now all but what had happened since, half wild with exhaustion and excitement, he had taken refuge at Doctor Chartley's.

"Don't touch the drink!" he muttered. "He thinks I have had D. T. Well, I did drink—brandy. I had some. Yes; I remember now—at the doctor's, and—Great Heavens!"

He paused, with his hands pressed to his forehead; and now the light had come back clearly.

He lay waiting till the nurse passed round again, and he signed to her to come to his side.

"You have sent to my sister?"

"Yes; a messenger has been sent."

"My clothes?" he said, in an eager whisper. "Where are they?"

"They have been taken care of quite safely."

"And the bag, and the belt—the cash-belt I had strapped round my waist?"

"I will make inquiries."

The nurse went away, and Mark Heath lay in an agony of spirit which he could hardly control till her return, to announce that he had nothing whatever upon him in the way of bag or money when found by the police.

Mark lay as if stunned till the messenger returned with the intelligence that Miss Heath had left the lodgings indicated; that the people there were new, and could give no information whatever.

"But you have other friends," said the nurse, as she looked down pityingly in the patient's agitated face.

"Yes," he said, "I have friends. Write for me to—"

He paused for a few moments, with a hysterical sob rising to his lips as he recalled how he had struggled to return to her wealthy, and had come back a beggar.

"Yes, to—"

The gently-spoken inquiry roused him, and he went on,

"To Miss Richmond—"

"Richmond?" said the nurse, looking up inquiringly as she took down the name in a little memorandum-book.

"Miss Richmond Chartley, 27 Ramillies Street, Queen's Square, Bloomsbury, to beg her to find and send my sister here."

The nurse smiled, and left him to his thoughts, which now came freely enough—too freely to help him to convalescence.

It was late in the evening when the nurse came to announce that there were visitors; and after a few grave firm words, bidding him be calm, she left him, and returned with Janet and Richmond, both trembling and agitated, to grasp his hands, and fight hard against the desire to throw themselves sobbing upon his breast.

The nurse remained, not from curiosity, but to watch over her patient, whom she had literally dragged from the grasp of death, while, after the first loving words, Mark Heath gazed at Richmond in a troubled way, and proceeded to tell of his adventures.

"But did you really bring back a bag of diamonds, Mark, or is it—"

"Fancy?" he said bitterly. "No; it is no fancy. I have been delirious, Jenny; but I am sane enough now. I had the bag of diamonds, and over a hundred pounds in gold, in a belt about my waist. Rich, darling, I was silent during these past two years; for I vowed that I would not write again till I could come back to you and say I have fulfilled my promise, and now I have come to you a beggar."

"Yes," said Richmond, laying her hand in his, as an ineffably sweet look of content beamed from her eyes in his, and there was tender yearning love in every tone of her sweet deep voice; "but you have come back alive after we had long mourned you as dead."

"Better that I had been," he said bitterly. "Better that that dark night's work had been completed than I should have come back a beggar."

Janet and Richmond exchanged glances, which with a sick man's suspicion he noted, and his brow contracted.

"They doubt me," he thought.

"But you have come back, Mark. We are young, and there is our life before us. I do not complain," said Richmond gently. "We must wait."

"Wait!" he said bitterly; and he uttered a low groan, which made the nurse approach.

"No, no," he said, "I will be quite calm."

The nurse drew back.

"Tell me, Mark," said Janet, with her pretty little earnest face puckered up. "Why did you not come straight to me? How stupid! Of course you did not know where, as you did not get my last letters."

"No, I have had no letters for a year. How could I, out in that desert?"

"But, Mark, you recollect being pursued by those men!"

"Yes, yes."

"You are sure it was not a dream?"

He looked at her almost fiercely.

"Dream? Could a man dream a thing like that?"

"Don't be cross with me, dear Mark," she said, laying her cheek against his. "It seems so strange, and you have been very, very ill. My own darling brother!"

It was not jealousy, but something very near akin, that troubled Rich as she stood there, with an intense longing to take her friend's place, after the long parting. But there was the recollection that their parting had not been the warm passionate embracing of lovers, only calm and full of the hope of what might be.

Janet continued:

"And you went late at night through a dreadful fog, and took refuge with a friend?"

"Yes," he said, with his features contracting, and a shudder passing through him, as he gazed furtively at Rich.

"And what can you recollect besides? Are you sure you had what you say—diamonds and money?"

"Yes, I am certain."

"I never wore diamonds," said Janet, with her pretty white forehead growing more puckered, "and I don't want any; but after being so poor, and with one's dearest friends so poor, and when it would make every one so happy, I should like you to find them again."

Mark uttered a low groan.

"But tell me, Mark, what else can you recollect?"

"Very little," he said. "It all seems misty; but I recollect drinking something."

"Brandy, Mark?"

"Yes; and afterwards a medicine that was to calm me, for I was half mad with excitement."

"Yes; go on."

"Then everything is confused: I seemed to fall asleep—a long restful sleep, that was broken by my taking a long journey."

"Yes, but that was dreaming, dear."

"Maybe," he said. "and then I was swimming—swimming for life—and then toiling on and on, a long weary journey under a hot sun to get my diamonds."

"Yes, dear, fever," said Janet, with the tears streaming down her cheeks. "Oh, Mark, what you have suffered! Rich, love, do you hear?"

"Yes—yes," cried Rich, who seemed to be roused from a strange dream, in which she was fighting to recall another of which she had a misty recollection —a dream that troubled her on the night she took the chloral, when half mad with pain.

"You have seen and borne so much, dear," said Janet piteously. "Was not all this about the bag of diamonds and those people a feverish dream?"

"Jenny, do you want to drive me mad?"

"My own dear old darling brother, no," she whispered caressingly; and once more that strange half-jealous feeling swept like a hot breath of wind across Rich, making her pale face flush. "I only want to make you see things rightly, and not fret about a fancy."

"I tell you it was no fancy," he said angrily; and

then, as the nurse held up a warning hand, "All right," he added, "I'll be calm."

"Say something to him, Rich," said Janet piteously.

Rich started, and then took Mark's hand. "You say that you went to the house of a friend?" she whispered.

"Ye—es," he replied hesitatingly.

"And that you partook of some medicine that was to make you sleep?"

He bowed his head slowly.

"And that your next clear recollection is of lying here, where you were brought after being found delirious by the police?"

"Yes, yes," he said impatiently.

"Robbed?"

"Stripped of everything," he said bitterly.

"It could not have been a friend, then, with whom you took refuge," said Rich.

Mark was silent.

"Must it not have been a dream?" said Janet in a whisper to her companion.

"No," said Rich aloud. "I think that all Mark recollects before he took this medicine must be true, and that this friend must have drugged him."

Mark drew a long, catching breath between his teeth.

"And robbed him while he slept."

Mark's breast rose and fell as if he were suffering some great emotion, and he stared at Rich wildly, his hand twitching and his lip quivering as he waited for her next speech, which seemed to crush him, as she asked in a clear firm voice.

"Who was the friend to whose house you went?"

He looked at her wildly, with the thoughts of the consequences of telling her that which he believed to be the truth—that Dr. Chartley—her father—the father of the woman he passionately loved—had drugged him—taken the treasure for which he had fought so hard, and then cast him forth feverish and delirious into the river to die. For he realized it now: he had been swimming; he could even recall the very plunge; he had been cast into the river to drown, and somehow he must have struggled out.

"Who was the friend, Mark?" she said again, in her calm firm way.

"Yes, who was it?" cried Janet, with her little lips compressed. "You are right, Rich. Some one did do this dreadful thing. Who was it, Mark?"

The sick man turned from her with a shudder, while she, all excitement now, pressed his hard hand.

"Tell us, Mark dear, that he may be punished, and made to restore what he has stolen."

"No, no!" he said excitedly; "I cannot tell you. I—I do not know."

"Try and recollect, Mark," said Rich gently; and she looked in his face with an appealing smile.

"No, no!" he gasped, as he shuddered again; "it is impossible. I—I do not know. And Heaven forgive me for my lie!" he muttered, as he sharply withdrew his hands, sank back upon his pillow, and covered his face.

"He must be left now," said the nurse firmly. "He is very weak, and your visit is proving painful. Say good-night to him. You can come to-morrow. He will be stronger after a night's rest."

"But—there is no danger?" whispered Rich, as she caught the sister's hand.

"No; the danger is past, but he must be kept quiet. Say good-night."

Janet bent down and kissed her brother lovingly; and as she drew back from his pallid drawn face, Rich took her place and held out her hand.

Mark caught it in both his, and there was an agonized look in his eyes.

"Rich," he whispered passionately, "I have come back to you a beggar, after fighting so hard. Heaven knows how hard, and what I am suffering for your sake. I cannot tell you more. I only say, believe in me and trust in me. Kiss me, my love—my love."

Richmond Chartley's pale face deepened, but she did not hesitate. There were patients here and there who lay witnessing the scene, and there were others present; but at that moment the world seemed very small, and they two the only living creatures it contained, as she bent down, passed her arm beneath his neck, and for the first time her lips met his.

"Rich—poor—what does it matter, Mark?" she whispered, with her warm breath seeming to caress his cheek. "You have come back to me, as it were, from the dead."

She drew down her veil as she rose from the parting, and the nurse's quick experienced eyes noted the restful happy look that had come over her patient's face.

"Good-bye," she said to the two visitors. "May I?"

Rich leaned forward, and the two women kissed.

"I had some one once whom I dearly loved. It

pleased God that he should die—for his country—trying to save a brother officer's life. Good-bye, dear. You are the best physician for him now. Come back soon."

Janet impulsively threw her arms about the sister's neck and kissed her.

"And I never thanked you for your care of my poor brother," she said. "But tell me, he is still a little wandering, is he not?"

"I could not help hearing all that passed," was the reply. "It was my duty to be present. I have, of course, had some experience of such cases, and I fear that he must have been drinking heavily in riotous company, and these ideas have become impressed upon his brain."

"And they are fancies?"

"I think so, but as he grows stronger these ideas will weaken, and you, his sister—and you——Ah, men are sometimes very weak, but to whom should they come for forgiveness when weak and repentant, if not to us?"

"But I won't believe my Mark has been going on as she hinted," said Janet, through her tears, as she walked away, weeping bitterly, and clinging tightly to Rich's arm.

"No; it is impossible," replied Rich; and with the feeling upon her that it was her duty to suffer for all in turn, and be calm and patient, she fought down her own longing to burst into a passionate fit of weeping, and walked on to resume her watch by her father's side, where he lay still insensible, as if in a sleep which must end in death.

"Rich dear, if it is true, and poor Mark was drugged

and robbed, the wretch who did it shall be brought to justice, shall he not?"

"Yes," said Rich, as she clasped the weeping girl to her breast.

And as she sat there in the silent chamber, through the dark watches of the night, at times a feeling of exultation and joy filled her breast, while at others a hot pang of rage shot through her, and she felt that she could slay the wretch who had raised a hand against him who had returned to her as from the dead.

CHAPTER XIII.

JANET IS HAUNTED.

A FORTNIGHT passed, and Mark was able to join his sister at her lodging, from which she was out all day.

It was very hard work, that lesson-giving at different houses, but little Janet trudged on from place to place, rarely ever traveling by omnibus unless absolutely obliged, so that she might economize and make her earnings help out her income of twenty-one pounds per annum.

Rather a small sum in London, but it was safe. Seven hundred pounds' worth of stock in the Three per Cents., and bringing in ten pounds ten shillings every half-year.

One evening, as she was returning on foot, walking very rapidly, so as to get back as soon as possible to Mark, her heart sank, and she felt faint in spirit as she thought of her future and its prospects. To go on teach, teach, teach, and try to make stupid girls achieve something approaching skill in handling their brushes, so that parents might be satisfied. For, poor girl, she found what most teachers do, that when a child does not progress, it is always the instructor's fault, not that of the disciple.

"I shall be better when I've had some tea," she said to herself, as the tears gathered in her eyes. "Why do I murmur so? Rich never complains, and her troubles are as great as mine. I ought to be glad and rejoice that poor Mark has come back safely, and—there he is again."

Janet's little heart beat wildly with fear as a tall muffled-up figure appeared from a doorway in the sombre-looking square into which she had turned from the street where she gave lessons three afternoons a week, and followed her at a short distance behind.

For two months past, evening after evening, that figure had been there, making her heart palpitate as she thought of what a weak, helpless little creature she was, and how unprotected in this busy world.

It was hard work to keep steadily on without looking round, without starting off at a run. Her breast seemed filled with that wild scream which she longed to utter, but dared not, telling herself that to seem afraid or to notice the figure was to invite assault.

"Oh, if Mark would only get well," she thought, "or if Rich could come and meet me!"

Then she called herself a coward, and stepped daintily on along the muddy street, wondering whether it would be possible to go by some other way, and so avoid this shadow which dogged her steps.

There was one way to get over it—to mention it to Rich, and ask her to bid Hendon wait for her and see her home. But that, she said, she would sooner die than do; so she had tried four different ways of reaching home, and always with the figure following her to the door of the house where she lodged, and where Mark sat waiting for her to come.

It was always the same: the muffled-up figure followed her closely, and kept on the same side of the way till she reached her door, when it crossed over, and waited till she went in, breathless and trembling.

Over and over again the little frightened girl tried to devise some plan, but all in vain; till this night of the foggy winter she was crossing the street, rejoicing that she was so near home, when there was a shout, a horse's hot breath was upon her cheek, and she was sent staggering sideways, and would have fallen had not the muffled-up figure been at hand, caught her in his arms, and borne her to the pavement, while the cab disappeared in the yellow mist.

"My own darling! Are you hurt?" he cried passionately.

"Hendon! You!" she panted.

"Yes, I," he said. "You are hurt!"

"No, no," she cried; "only frightened. The horse struck my shoulder. But—but was it you who followed me every night all the way home?"

"Yes," he said, coldly now, "you knew it was."

"I did not," she retorted angrily; and then in half hysterical tones, "how dare you go on frightening me night after night like this? It has been horrible. You have made me ill."

"Made you ill?" he said. "How could I let you go about all alone these dark evenings? I was forbidden to talk to you as I wished, but there was no reason why I should not watch over you. How's Mark?"

"Getting better," said Janet, drawing a breath of relief at her companion's sudden change in the conversation; for she felt that had he continued in that same sad reproachful strain she must have hung upon his arm, and sobbed and thanked him for his chivalrous conduct. There was something, too, so sweet in the feeling that he must love her very dearly in spite of all the rebuffs he had received; and somehow as they walked on, a gleam of sunny yellow came through the misty grays and dingy drabs with which from her mental color-box she had been tinging her future life. There was even a dash of ultramarine, too—a brighter blue than her eyes —and her heart began to beat quite another tune.

"May I come and walk home with you every night?" said Hendon at last, as, after repeated assurances that she was not hurt, they stopped at last at the street door.

"No," she said decidedly; and her little lips were tightly compressed, so that they should not give vent to a sob.

"How cruel you are, Janet!"

"For trying to do what is right," she said firmly. "What would your sister say if, after all that has passed, I were to be so weak?"

"May I follow you at a distance, as I have done all this time?" he pleaded.

"No. You have only frightened me almost to

death," she replied. "Will you come up and see poor Mark?"

"Not to-night," he said bitterly; "I couldn't bear it now. Janet, if I go to the bad, it won't be all my fault. I know I'm a weak fellow, but with something to act as ballast, I should be all right. What have I done that you should be so cold?"

For answer, Janet held out her hand.

"Good-night, Mr. Chartley," she said quietly; but he did not take the hand, only turned away, walking rapidly along the street, while, fighting hard to keep from bursting into a violent fit of sobbing, Janet hurried up to her room, to find her brother looking haggard and wild as he slowly paced the floor.

CHAPTER XIV.

MARK HEATH IN THE DARK.

"No—NO—no!" Always the same determined answer to the declarations of Janet that some steps should be taken to investigate the affairs of the night on which her brother had first reached London.

"No," he said; "I will have nothing done. Let me get well, and away from here. "I've escaped with my life."

"And what will you do, Mark?" asked Janet, as she sat by his side.

"Try again," he said. "But I must first get well."

He had heard that the doctor was ill, but everything else had been kept from him, till one evening, as he was seated by the fire at Janet's neat little lodgings, and his sister was called down to see a visitor.

She had a suspicion of who it was, and found Richmond waiting.

"Come up and see him."

Richmond hesitated.

"I must not stay long," she said. "My father frets for me if I am away."

"And I am situated almost the same. Mark does not like to be left. Come up, dear, and help me to persuade him that he ought to employ the police."

"No, no! don't talk of them," said Richmond, with a shudder. "I want the horror at our house forgotten, and they keep reminding me that the law does not sleep."

"Why, Rich, how strangely you talk!"

"Strangely, dear! No. Only it comes back like a nightmare ever since that terrible affair, so soon as it is mentioned. I seem to be wandering about the house in misery, fever, and pain, trying to see through a mist that I cannot penetrate. I don't know how it is or what it means, but I have this horrible thought troubling me, that I came down that night to go to the surgery, and that I saw something."

"Saw something! Saw what?"

"Ah! that is what I cannot tell," said Rich with a shudder. "I was better this morning, and more hopeful. My poor father seemed a little clearer in his mind, but the past is all a blank to him."

"He knew me, dear, when I came yesterday."

"Oh, yes! and he knows me well enough. He talks sensibly about what is going on around him; but that night when he was struck down, the blows seemed to break away the connection between the present and the past. The physician, who has seen him, says very little, but I can see that he considers the case hopeless."

"Oh, don't say that, dear! We must all hope. I hope to be something better some day than a poor teacher. Come up now, and help me to persuade Mark to have in the police."

"No, no!" cried Rich hastily.

"Why not, dear?" Think what it means if it is true about the diamonds, and we could get them back."

"But it cannot be true, Janet; and as to the police, they make me shudder. They were at our house this morning to see Hendon, and with him my father, to try whether they could revive his memory, and get hold of a clue to those men who came to our house that night, and they have found out nothing. They say they are straining every nerve now to find that poor boy. They think he must hold the clue."

"I think I could find it all out if I tried," said Janet. "Had your father any enemies?"

Richmond shook her head.

"Any one to whom he owed money?"

Richmond started, and her thoughts reverted to Poynter.

"No, no, no—impossible! Let it rest, dear. I have thought over it, till it nearly drives me mad!" she cried excitedly.

"It is very strange," continued Janet musingly. "I don't like to let it rest, and there is our trouble, too. Rich dear, has it ever occurred to you that it must have been the same night when poor Mark was found wandering about?"

"No!"

"Yes, dear. I have calculated it out from what the hospital sister told me. It was the same night."

Rich looked at her wonderingly.

"It was, dear," continued Janet. "While you had that horror at home, I was sleeping here comfortably, and poor Mark was wandering about the cruel streets half wild."

Rich made a gesture to her friend to be silent, and Janet passed her arm about her waist, to lead her upstairs, but with the full determination to try and make some investigation. For though there were times when the thought of her brother having brought home a bag of diamonds seemed mythical, and the birth of his diseased imagination—especially as he never named them now—at other times visions of comparative wealth had come to her, in the midst of which she seemed to see herself with Hend on, and her old companion and her brother happily looking on.

Mark was seated gazing moodily at the fire as Richmond entered with his sister, and he rose to take her hands, and lead her to a chair.

But somehow both seemed constrained and troubled by thoughts which they kept from each other.

"I know," said Janet to herself, "it's that dreadful money which is keeping them apart, and if I don't do something, Mark will be going off again to seek his fortune, and it is like condemning poor Rich and himself to a life of misery and waiting."

She sat working, but furtively watching the others all the while.

"This poverty is killing us all," she said to herself at last. "and I will speak. It may be true, and he shall do something to find out."

"Mark dear," she said aloud, "I have something to say."

"Indeed! Well, what is it?"

"I've come to the conclusion that, now you are better, you ought to speak out like a man, and—"

"Stop!" he said hoarsely.

"No, Mark, I shall not stop," cried Janet decidedly. "You say that you went to a friend's house that night with all your money and—and treasure."

"Girl! will you be silent?" he cried savagely.

"No," said Janet, laughing. "I want you to see this matter as I do. Whoever this man is, he ought to be forced to give up what he must have stolen from you. If you will not stir, I shall."

"You will?"

"Yes; I shall take counsel with Hendon again."

"Again?" almost yelled Mark.

"Yes, sir, again. We have spoken over the matter together, and he agrees that the police ought to be seen, and that you must make this friend give up what he has taken."

"You'll drive me mad, Janet. Hendon thinks this?"

"Yes; and we are going to do it at once, for the sake of you and Rich."

"You shall not stir!" cried Mark fiercely.

"Why not?" interposed Rich, taking his hand. "I think with my brother and Janet now, much as I dislike these investigations."

"You think so—you?" cried Mark wildly.

"Yes. Why not?" said Rich. "Mark dear, why

should you flinch from speaking out?" You can have no unworthy motive."

"Unworthy motive? No," he said bitterly. "I give up everything to spare another."

"Then you shall not," said Janet firmly. "Your duty is to Richmond here; your promised wife."

"Yes," said Mark moodily; "my duty is to Rich here, my promised wife."

"And yet for the sake of some unworthy wretch, you make her suffer—yes, sir, and me too. Why, Rich, dear Rich, what is the matter?"

She flew to her friend's side, and caught her hands; for Rich had started from her chair, looking wildly from one to the other, as, struggling as it were from out of a confused mist, how revived she could not tell, there came back to her, memory by memory, the scenes of that terrible night. Yes: she remembered now, though it still seemed like a dream—a fragmentary, misty dream.

Yes, that was the clue! Janet had said it was upon that same night that Mark had returned—had been found senseless in the streets.

"Don't, don't speak to me for a minute!" she cried, as she fought hard to recall everything—the maddening pain that night, the visit to the surgery, the chloral she had obtained and taken, and then that strange wild sleep.

Yes; she recalled it now. She dreamed she had come down to fetch something else from the surgery to allay the agony she suffered, and that the door was locked, and that she had heard voices—her father's voice, Mark's voice—yes, it was Mark's voice; and she had stood there trembling till it died away; and that formed part of her dream.

But now the voice was here in this room, and he caught her hand with a wildly suspicious look in his eye.

"What are you thinking?" he said.

She turned upon him sharply.

"The name of your friend with whom you took refuge that night?" she said; and her eyes flashed as she gazed searchingly in his.

He dropped her hand, and turned away, with his lips compressed and face contracted.

"Mark," she cried, " why do you not speak? Where did you go that night when you returned?"

He looked at her for a moment, and then turned away again. "I do not know," he said hoarsely.

"It is not true," cried Rich. "You must speak now. It was to our house you came."

"What!"

"I remember now. I heard your voice. You were with my father—in the surgery."

"Rich," he said, almost savagely, as he caught her wrist, "think of what you are saying!"

"Rich dear, don't say that!" cried Janet piteously.

"I know what I am saying," she said excitedly; and though her face was calm, it was evident that she was suffering terribly.

"No, no," he cried; "no, dear, you are wrong."

"No, Mark, I am right: you told us you took refuge with a friend—that friend was my father."

"What! Rich, do you know what you are saying —do you know what this means if the police should hear?"

"Yes," she cried; the clearing up of a terrible

mystery; perhaps the restoration of all that you have lost."

"Janet, is she mad?" cried Mark. "Do you not see what all this means?"

Janet shook her head with a helpless look on her face.

"Then I will tell you," he thundered: "it means ruin—misery to us all. Girl, for pity's sake, be silent! Rich, dear Rich, I love you with a man's first strong love. Have I not slaved for you all these years, to win you for my own true wife? Don't—don't raise this up between us. What is poverty to such a shadow as this?"

"I do not understand you," she cried; "but it is true. You did come to my father's house that night."

He gazed at her in blank despair.

"Why do you look at me like that? Do you not see the light?"

"The light!" he cried, with a bitter laugh. "I see you—the woman I love—trying to force me into a position which I would sooner die than hold. Hush, for mercy's sake! No, no, no!" he muttered; and then aloud, "Call it a lie, or a desperate man's last cry for help. I did not come to your father's house that night."

Rich gazed at him in blank astonishment for the moment, and then she flung her arms about his neck, and with her eyes close to his, she cried.

"What are you thinking—that it was my father who drugged and robbed you, or my brother? Oh, Mark?"

She seemed to throw him off as she stepped back,

her pale face flushing, and a look of indignant anger in her eyes.

"What does this mean?" cried Janet; but her words fell unheeded.

"Shame on you! You are silent. How could you think this thing?"

"Heaven help me!" groaned Mark. "And I fought so hard!"

By a sudden revulsion of feeling, Rich turned to him again, and with her sweet rich voice, full of the agony of her heart, she caught his hands.

"How could you think it of him, Mark! My poor gentle-hearted father! Do you not see? Did you not tell us that you were hunted from place to place by those men?"

"Rich, my darling," groaned Mark, as he strained her to his breast, "do you not see that you are digging a gulf between us, and that you will soon be standing on the other side, shrinking from me in abhorrence as the man who has brought this charge against your father? And God knows how I have striven to bear all in silence!"

"But, Mark—"

"Rich, it is your doing, not mine!" he cried wildly. "What are the diamonds to the loss of you?"

"But, Mark," she cried impetuously, "this is madness. You suspect him. You shall speak now—you shall. You have thought my father did this thing?"

"You drag it from me," he groaned. "I do."

"Oh, shame!" cried Richmond, shrinking from him; "to suspect the poor old man, who nearly died in your defence."

"What!" cried Mark.

"Whom we found struck down bleeding, and whom

I am neglecting now, when he is hovering almost between life and death—neglecting that I might come to him whom I thought the soul of chivalry and faith."

"Stop!" cried Mark, in a harsh voice, as he released Rich, who struggled from him, and stood with his hands pressed to his eyes. "Janet, I have been off my head. I seem to think wildly now and then. Do I hear her aright, or am I still confused? What does she say?"

"I—I don't quite know myself," faltered Janet, bursting into tears.

"And yet I seem to understand," cried Mark excitedly. "Rich dearest, speak to me again. Your father found—struck down—in my defence?"

"Yes, that is what I said," replied Rich coldly.

"Struck down in my defence. I did not know of this."

"You—you knew he was very ill," sobbed Janet.

"Yes; but I knew no more."

"How could we tell you when you were nearly dead?" sobbed Janet; "and the doctor said you were not to be troubled in any way."

Mark Heath stood as if dazed for a few minutes, striving to think coherently, and master the delusion under which he had been suffering.

"Rich," he cried at last, "for God's sake, tell me all!"

CHAPTER XV.

A PHYSICIAN UNHEALED.

JAMES POYNTER sat polishing his hat with his handkerchief, and staring at Hendon with a contraction, half smile, half grin, upon his face.

"I tell you I can't pay you. You forced the money upon me."

"I forced it on you! Come, that's a good one! Now, are you going to pay?"

"You know I can't, Poynter. You must wait."

"Not likely. "Well, I must have my money, and what your father owes me too."

"I have only your word that he does owe you money, James Poynter."

"All right, Mr. Hendon; go on. Insult me. The more patient I am the more advantage you take. Ask him if he don't."

"Ask him?" said the young man bitterly; "you know his mind is as good as gone."

"Is it as bad as that?" said Poynter, with assumed pity, but his eyes twinkling with eagerness, as he wound the handkerchief round and round.

"Bad? yes. Millington, our best man, saw him yesterday, and he says nothing but an operation and raising the bone pressing on the brain will relieve him; and at his age he would not be responsible for the result."

Poynter drew a breath full of satisfaction, and smiled at his polished hat.

"Well, I think the operation ought to be performed, so as to bring him to his senses again. Poor old boy! He does seem queer. I asked him—"

"What, you spoke to that poor old man about your cursed debt!" cried Hendon furiously.

"Of course I did. Cursed debt, indeed! Why, I've behaved as well as a man could behave. Look-ye here, do you want me to sell you up?"

Hendon uttered an ejaculation, and, writhing under his impotence, he began pacing the old dining-room, while with a show of proprietorship James Poynter set down his hat, put his handkerchief therein, took out his case, and selected a cigar.

"Have a weed?" he said, nipping the end of the one he was about to smoke.

"D—n you, and your cigars too!" cried the young man furiously.

"Thank ye, cub!" said Poynter, lighting up. "There, you won't make me waxy. I'm a true friend in disguise. Ah, this is one of a noo lot I bought. Have one, old man."

Hendon made a fierce gesticulation, and scowled in the grinning face.

"How long are you going to stop here?" he said.

"Long as I like. P'raps I shall have the house done up, and come and live here."

"What?"

"Ah! what indeed! Suppose I bought the lease of the governor? What have you got to say to that?"

Hendon glared at him wildly.

"How's the little angel—Janet?"

Hendon's hands clenched, and he ground his teeth, while Poynter laughed at him.

"So the big brother's out of the hospital; got over his D. T., and lodging with his sister, eh?"

Hendon made no reply.

"Come, old chap," continued Poynter, "have a cigar, and do try and be sensible. I don't want to do nothing hard, but of course a man must fight for his own hand. I haven't come here to sell you up, but to bring you to your senses, like the friend I always was. Now look here, Hendon, this brother seems to be as loose a fish as a girl could have for a relation; but Miss Heath's as smart a little lass as e'er stepped—"

"Have the goodness to leave Miss Heath's name alone, sir."

"Waxy again. Now look here, Hendon, I'm a rich man. Suppose I say to you, my lad, look out for a snug little practice; I'll lend you the money—can't afford to give it—buy the practice, and marry Janet. Isn't that being a friend?"

Hendon went on pacing the room.

"Sulky, eh? All right: answer me this, then. Shouldn't I make your sister a better husband than this Mark Heath? Come, be sensible; take me upstairs to see her. Now, at once. Let me make things pleasant for all of you. What's the good of being enemies, when we might be friends?"

"Friends!"

"Better than being master and slave, eh, Hendon, my lad? Borrower slave to the lender, eh?"

"Ah!" ejaculated Hendon.

"Come, come, you're sensible now. Take me upstairs, and let's have it out with Rich."

"With Rich!" cried Hendon passionately.

"There, don't you be so cocky, young man. I

don't call your Janet, Jenny. Yes, with Rich; my own dear darling Rich. There! How do you like that? Now then, let's get it over."

"My sister is not at home."

"Then we'll go up and see the old man; and let's hear what he'll say to it all. He won't deny that he's in my debt."

"Poor old fellow, no," groaned Hendon to himself.

"I say," said Poynter, turning grave, "where's Rich? She hasn't gone to see that sailor chap?"

"I don't know whom you mean by 'sailor chap,'" said Hendon bitterly.

"Then I'll tell you," he said. "I mean Mark Heath, and I've got a theory of my own about him."

"Curse you and your theories!" cried Hendon fiercely.

"Yes, and bless me and my money," said Poynter, laughingly.

"Stop! Where are you going?"

"This is my house, or as good as mine," said Poynter; "and I'm going up to see my poor old father-in-law to be. I don't think he's properly seen to, and I mean to have him off down to the seaside, to try and pull him round. Coming?"

Hendon was so much staggered by his visitor's cool insolence that Poynter was at the foot of the staircase before he thought to follow; and then, feeling that this man had a hold upon him that he dared not shake off, he followed him upstairs, and into the sparely-furnished front drawing-room into which the doctor had been lying all through his illness.

He was seated where he could see the window,

and his handsome face looked vacant and strange as he turned his head to Elizabeth, who was waiting on him in her mistress's absence.

"Is that Rich?" he said feebly.

"No, doctor, it's me, come for a bit of advice," cried Poynter. "Here," he said, turning to the maid, as he whisked his handkerchief round his hat, "you be off."

Elizabeth left the room, wiping her eyes, and Poynter sat down beside the doctor, and shook hands.

"Why," I ought to feel your pulse now, and not you mine," he said boisterously.

"Glad to see you, Mr. Poynter. Pretty well, thank you. Is my Rich coming?"

"To be sure she is, old boy. Now, I just want a cosy chat with you about Rich."

"About Rich? Yes, yes."

"You remember how I proposed for her?"

The doctor looked at him blankly, and shook his head. "Is Rich coming, Hendon?" he said.

"Yes, father; she is here," he cried; for there was the sound of wheels, and running to the window, he smiled grimly as he saw who descended from the cab.

"Might have stopped a little longer," grumbled Poynter to himself. "It don't matter; the game's mine now. D——n!"

He started from his seat as he saw Rich enter the room, closely followed by Mark Heath and Janet, to whom Hendon hurried with outstretched hands, and after a little hesitation, two little dark well-manded gloves and their contents were placed in his strong grasp.

"Dearest father," said Rich softly, as she hurried to the old man's side.

"Ah," he said, taking her hands, and fondling them, while a brighter smile came into his pleasant vacant face; "that's better—that's better. Here's Mr.—Mr.—Mr.—"

"Poynter, doctor," said that individual, glad of an opportunity to remove his eyes from Mark's, which were gazing at him rather inimically.

"Yes, yes, Mr. Poynter come to see us, Rich."

"And I have come to see you too, doctor," said Mark. "You remember me?"

The doctor looked up at him keenly, and then shook his head, and, with a troubled look in his eyes.

"No," he said. "No—no—no."

"Hah!" ejaculated Poynter, with a smile of satisfaction.

"Mark Heath, father dear," said Rich gently. "Don't you remember Mr. Heath, who went to the Cape?"

"Heath?" said the doctor; "Heath—Heath? No—no," he added thoughtfully. "Glad to see Mr. Heath. Friend of Hendon's?" His words were calm, but he seemed to wince.

"No, doctor: I'm Hendon's friend," said Poynter, with a laugh; and he gave his hat a loving wipe.

"Yes, Mr. Poynter. You came to see me the day before yesterday. I remember—remember. I prescribed—"

"That's right, sir; that's right," cried Poynter, with one of his horse laughs.

"Is this man going, Hendon?" whispered Mark impatiently.

"No, Mr. Mark Heath, he ain't," said Poynter fiercely. "Speak lower if you don't want people to hear; we've got sharp ears in the City, and I'm not going."

"No, no; Mr. Poynter has come to see me," said the doctor, gazing in a frightened way at Mark. "Don't go, Mr. Poynter. It's very dull here."

"I'm not going, doctor. It's all right," said the unwelcome visitor. "You're going to set me right."

"You'll excuse me—Mr. Poynter, I think," said Mark; "but I have some private business to transact with Dr. Chartley."

"Yes, I'll excuse you as much as you like. I've got private business with Doctor Chartley, too."

"Why, Mark," cried Hendon, "have you found out anything about your loss?"

"Yes. No. Well, yes; I have learned something," cried Mark excitedly, and he glanced again angrily at Poynter.

But the latter's unwelcome presence seemed to be ignored by all, in the intense excitement of the moment. For Rich threw herself upon her knees at her father's feet, and took his hands.

"Father dear," she said gently, "I want you to try and remember something."

"Yes, my dear, yes—certainly, certainly," said the old man, bending down to kiss her tenderly.

"That night, you know, when—when you were taken ill."

"Yes, my love, that night I was taken ill? Was I taken ill?"

"Yes, dear; but you are nearly well now. Do you remember Mr. Heath coming? Try and remember, dear."

Poynter's face grew convulsed and angry, and he seemed to be looking about for some moral weapon with which to attack his enemy, but contented himself with a whisk of his handkerchief around his hat.

"Heath, dear? This is Mr. Heath, you say—Heath?" and the doctor's face grew troubled.

"Yes, yes. Do you remember his coming to see you?"

The doctor looked from one to the other, and shook his head.

"Oh, father, dear father, for my sake try!" cried Rich. "Do you not remember his coming to you?"

The doctor put his hand to his head, and looked wildly round.

"No," he said at last. "No, I don't think I have seen Mr. Heath before;" but the wild look was still in his eyes.

"Don't say that, doctor," said Mark, taking his hand. "You have forgotten. Don't you remember? That dreadful foggy night. I came to you, and you let me into the surgery?"

"Yes, dear, you recollect," cried Rich, piteously.

"I was utterly exhausted, and worn out—very much excited," continued Mark. "You took me into the consulting-room, and I lay down upon the sofa. You gave me brandy, and some narcotic."

"Brandy and a narcotic," said the doctor, smiling; "rather a strange mixture. Did I?"

"Yes; you recollect now?" said Mark eagerly.

The doctor looked at him intently, and then at Rich; but ended by shaking his head slowly.

"No," he said, "I do not recollect."

"All this is maddening!" muttered Mark, "just

when one's hopes were reviving, and there was a chance of discovering something. Doctor," he continued excitedly, "try and recollect."

"Yes, dear, for Mark Heath's sake, try," continued Rich; and Poynter ground his teeth, as he felt what he would give to evoke the same interest for himself.

"I will try, my love," said the doctor blandly. "Of course."

"Then you remember I told you I had just come from the Cape; that I had a bag of diamonds in my breast?"

Poynter uttered a sneering laugh, which made Heath wince, and turn upon him wrathfully.

"Diamonds? did you say a bag of diamonds?" said the doctor.

"Yes, yes; you remember."

"Was it not a very unsafe place to carry diamonds?"

"Yes, of course it was; but I could trust no one but myself. You remember then, doctor?"

Dr. Chartley paused for a few moments, and shook his head again.

"No," he said blandly, "I do not remember. Diamonds, you say?"

"Yes, yes, diamonds!"

"I hope they were not lost," said the doctor simply.

"Yes; lost, lost!" cried Mark frantically. "The night you were struck down!"

"Here, hold hard!" cried Poynter sharply. "Look here, Mr. Mark Heath, you came here that night?"

"Why do you interfere, sir?"

"Never mind. P'r'aps I know something."

"You know something?"

"P'r'aps so. You say you came here—late?"

"Yes, very late."

"That night the doctor was struck down?"

"Yes; but why do you ask?"

"Because, you scoundrel, we've got the clue at last. You were the man!"

So sudden was the charge that Mark literally staggered back, and, weak from his illness, he gasped, and looked to a superficial observer as much like a guilty man as ever recoiled from a sudden denunciation. But as a wave of the advancing tide merely retires to gain fresh force, Mark Heath recovered himself.

"You scoundrel!" he cried; and he would have sprung at Poynter's throat, but for the restraining arm of Janet and Hendon.

"Scoundrel yourself!" cried Poynter savagely. "Look at his face! Here—the police!"

He strode towards the door, upon which at that moment there was a loud tapping; and before he could reach it, Bob stood in the opening, very rough of head, very ragged, and looking as if he had not been washed since he was missed.

CHAPTER XVI.

BOB IS EXPLANATORY.

"HERE, boy," cried Poynter, "quick! Fetch a policeman. Half-a-crown."

He thrust his hand into his pocket, but at that moment even that outrageously large sum had not the slightest effect upon the boy, who looked quickly round from one to the other till his eyes lit upon Mark, at whom he rushed with the action of a well-trained dog, seizing him by the arm and breast of his coat, and clinging tightly.

"I've got him," he said shrilly. "Fetch the perlice. I've got him, Miss Rich; I see him come that night."

Poynter raised his fist, and struck it into his open hand.

"I knew it!" he cried. "I knew I was right! Now, Mr. Mark Heath, what have you got to say?"

"Hendon, lad, lay hold of this boy. He's mad."

"No, I ain't," cried Bob. "Had 'nuff to make me, though."

"Let go, you dog!" roared Mark.

"All right, I'm a-going to," said the boy, shrinking away as Rich came to him.

"Bob," she cried, "what is this you're saying?"

"Well, I d' know, Miss," he said, scratching his head; "and I don't think now it weer him. But I'll sweer he come and told the doctor as the perlice or some one was arter him."

"Yes, boy, yes; I did come, but you were not there."

"Worn't I? Yes, I was," said the boy, grinning. "I see you come, and you'd got one o' them long-tail ulcers and a broad-brimmed hat; and the doctor— I say, Miss, is he better?"

"Yes, yes, Bob; but pray go on."

"I am glad the gov'ner's better. It scared me. I thought he was a dead 'un."

The boy looked round, and gave everybody a confidential nod, including "'Lisbeth," who was standing at the door, crying, and smiling with satisfaction by turns.

"But you say you saw me come!" cried Mark, while Poynter stood looking on in triumph.

"See you come? Course I did. I know'd you d'reckly, but I don't think it was you as did it."

"No, boy, it was not I. But where were you?"

"Wheer was I? Ah! you wouldn't know. I was afraid o' the doctor-dropping on to me for being there, and I skipped into the bone box."

"What!" cried Hendon.

"I did, sir, 'strue as goodness. There's lot's o' room, and I could just lift up the lid and peep, and that's how I see him come,"

"You young rascal?" muttered Hendon; while the doctor sat quietly smiling, as if it were something got up for his special amusement.

"Then the doctor he took you into his room, and you had some bran'-water hot. I smelt it. And then he come and got down one o' the bottles, and misked you up a dollop o' physic; and I heared you both a-buzzing away, and talking about wheer you'd been. The doctor kep' coaxing of you, like, to go to sleep, and somehow that sent me off."

"What! in that box with those—"

"Oh, yes, I don't mind them. I often nips in there when any one's coming."

"Did you hear anything else, Bob?" said Rich excitedly, as she held the boy's hand.

"Not till some one else come, and knocked two or three times; and I was going to answer the door, when the doctor come and turned down the gas, and then I lay still, and heard him putting the physic bottles away afore he'd let 'em in; didn't you, sir?"

The doctor smiled, and shook his head.

"Why, I heared you!" said the boy reproachfully; "and then you turns up the gas again, and I lifts the lid a bit, and sees it was two men and an accident."

"An accident?"

"Yes, Miss, a chap as they said had been run over; and they brings him in, and puts him on the cushin a top o' the box I was in; and I lay still and listens, for I says as it was a good chance to hear a operation, if I couldn't see one."

"Go on, boy; go on."

"All right, sir. Well, as I listens—oh, it was good! The chap groans and hollers about his chest, and then he makes no end of fuss, and the doctor says he'll soon be all right; and then—*whoosh!—croosh!* I hears as if some one had been hit, and a big fall —*quelck!* Then I lay very still, for I was scared. I heard some one get off the box, and a lot o' whisperings, and I dursn't move, for fear they should know I were there. But when I did peep, and lifted the lid softly, there was the doctor lying close to the box, on his face, and I thought he was dead.

"That give me a turn, Miss," continued the boy, after moistening his lips, for his voice had become husky, "and I don't think I knowed what happened till I heerd a skeary kind o' noise, and a loud sort o' whop in the 'sulting-room; and then the door was opened, and I see the light shining on you a-lying on the sofa—you, sir—sleep or shamming, and a man in there too, a-lying down, and—and—I—I can't help it, Miss—I ain't had much to eat lately, and I —I—"

Poor Bob let himself sink in a heap upon the floor, covered his face with his hands, and burst into a fit of sobbing.

There was another fit of sobbing heard, for grimy-faced Elizabeth rushed forward, plumped down beside the boy, and took his head to her breast, to rock him to and fro.

"Poor boy!" said Rich softly, and she took his hand.

The touch was like magic; for Bob lifted up his dirty tearful face, all smiles.

"It's all right, Miss: I'm on'y a bit upset. Only let me get into the surgery again, and I knows what to take to put me right."

"Can you tell us any more, my lad?" said Mark kindly.

"Course I can, sir; not much, though, for I dunno what come over me. I see them two a-lying about, and as something horrid was the matter, and I come over all wet and sick; and then I don't remember any more till I seemed to wake up with a headache, and couldn't make out what it all meant;

and when I could I lifted up the box-lid, and put out my hand, and felt to try if it was fancy. But there was the doctor lying on his face, and though all was very quiet, I knowed the other dead 'un must be in the 'sulting-room, and I lay there 'fraid to move, and all of a pruspiration."

"Did you hear anything else?" said Rich eagerly.

"Yes, Miss; I heared the window broke, and you come, and the perliceman, and I heared all you said; but I dursn't move, for fear the perlicemen should think I did it—the perlice is such wunners, you know; and last of all, I hears the perliceman begin hunting about, and I got scared again, and tried to hide; and jus' as I picks up that there white skull, and was trying whether I couldn't get lower, he opens the lid, and bangs it down."

"Should you know the men again?" asked Mark eagerly.

"Dunno, sir. You see it was all foggy like, and they was wropped up; but I should know 'em if I heerd 'em speak."

Mark uttered an ejaculation full of disappointment, and signed to the boy to go on.

"Well, sir, that's all; only I waited till no one was there; and then I lifted the lid and crep out of the box; and it was very horrid, for there was the dead chap in the nex' room, and I kep' thinking he'd come after me, or them others would; and I was that scared, I crawled along the passage, and down-stairs, and then sat and shivered, list'ning to you folks talking, and something in my head going buzz."

"Why did you not come to us?" said Rich kindly.

"I did want to, Miss, but I dursn't. I was 'fraid 'bout what you'd say; and there was the perliceman too, and I'd no business to be there. I d'know, only I was very frightened, and didn't hardly know what I did. I never see anybody dead afore."

"Well, what did you do then?"

"Waited a bit, Miss, and then got out in the area, nipped over the rails, and went home and told mother."

"But one minute," cried Mark, pressing his hand to his breast; "did you—did you hear anything said about—about diamonds?"

"Yes," cried the boy. "I heared one on 'em say, 'Be cool, and the diamonds are ours.'"

Mark uttered a groan. His last hope was crushed; and the boy went on:

"Mother said she know'd no good 'ud come of my being at a doctor's, and that it all meant body-snatching and 'section, and that I shouldn't get into trouble for no one. She said if I stopped I should be took up by the perlice; and I was scared enough, and did as she said, and she took me with her down in the country."

"In the country?" cried Hendon. "Where did you go?"

"I d'know," said the boy. "Everywhere's, I think. Tramping about, and sleeping in workusses; and it's been very cold and mis'able, and I'm very fond o' the old woman; only somehow—"

"Well, Bob, why do you stop?" said Hendon.

"Dunno, sir," said the boy, looking very hard at Rich's white hand. "I wouldn't ha' done it, on'y she was took bad, and they put her in one of the workus 'firmaries, and wouldn't let me stop along with her. They shoved me in a school as was all whitewash, with a lot more boys; and I got in a row with some on 'em, and we had a fight, and the master caned me, and I hooked it; and please, Miss, mayn't I stay?"

CHAPTER XVII.

A JAR WRONGLY LABELLED.

James Poynter blustered and threatened; but the only proceedings he took were the sending of threatening letters to Hendon—letters which Mark advised him to throw into the fire.

"Wait," said the latter one evening, "and let him develop his attack; we should only weaken ourselves by going out to meet him."

"But if he really has claims on my father, and seizes this place?"

"Then, my lad, you and I must set to, and see if it is not possible for us to join hands and get together another home for your father and sister—one, perhaps, that, if small, might be made happy till I came back."

"Came back?" said Janet, who had accompanied her brother to the doctor's that evening.

"Yes, dear," said Mark. "I have not said a word to a soul; but I'm going back to the Cape by the next boat."

"To try your luck again?" said Hendon quickly.

"To try my luck again," replied Mark; and he glanced at Rich, who was seated at work with Janet, while the doctor looked on, and smiled placidly at both in turn.

Rich turned very pale; but she did not speak.

"I have no prospects here," continued Mark;

"and out yonder I have faith in making some progress. I shall tempt my fate again."

"And if I could only feel sure that those we left behind would be safe," cried Hendon, "I'd go with you."

Janet's eyes lit up, and it was a look more of encouragement than blame which she directed at her lover.

"You, Hendon?" said Mark, smiling.

"Yes; I want to get away, and begin differently. I'm—there, look here, Mark Heath; with a strong-minded chap like you, I know I could get on, doctoring or diamond-digging, or something of that kind. Hallo, what is it?"

"Letter, sir."

"Letter? Why didn't the boy bring it up?"

"He's a-dusting the surgery, sir," replied the maid, who seemed to have been engaged upon some cleansing business in which she had been worsted.

"For you, Hendon," said Rich, who had taken the letter. "Is it from the hospital?"

"No, it isn't from the hospital," said Hendon quietly, as he knit his brow over the correctly-written formal letter, in which a firm of solicitors respectfully informed him that unless certain sums due on dishonored bills were paid to them in a specified time, they were instructed by their client, Mr. James Poynter, to take immediate proceedings for the recovery of the debt.

"Mark, old chap, the attack has begun;" and Hendon handed the letter to the former, who read it through.

"Let's go down stairs," he said. "I want to talk to you."

"Is anything wrong?" said Janet anxiously.

"Nothing fresh, my dear," replied Mark: "Hendon and I are going to chat over matters. We shall be up again soon."

"But is the news very bad?" said Rich.

"No: on the whole good," replied Mark; and he and Hendon went down-stairs, and were going into the dining-room, but the gas was lit in the surgery, and they went there, to find Bob going over the bottles, and, after a careful polish, putting them back.

"Be off for a bit, my boy," said Hendon; "or—no; go on with your work."

He took a match from a box on a shelf, and lit the consulting-room lamp.

"Here," he said, "room's chilly; we may as well have a pipe over it."

Mark nodded, and they smoked for a few minutes in silence.

"Why did you say that was good news?" said Hendon at last.

"Because the enemy shows his hand."

"Shows his hand? How?"

"If he had any claim upon your father, he would have attacked him first. He has no claim. It was an empty boast."

"So much the better," cried Hendon. "Well, that settles it. I shall go off with you."

Mark smoked in silence.

"If you'll have me. But I say, old fellow, do you quite give up the diamonds?"

"Quite."

"You said you had been to the police again, yesterday."

"Yes, and they say they think they can lay their hands upon the men when they try to sell."

"Well, then, there is hope."

"Not a bit. They are cooling down. "I don't think they have much faith in my story; and, besides, the matter is growing stale. They have a dozen more things on the way. Hendon, my lad, you love my sister?"

"On my—"

"That will do. I believe it; but neither yo nor I can marry for years to come. You shall go w ⸺h me, and we *will* come back well enough off to make those two our wives."

"But Poynter's debt? He'll have me arrested before I can leave the country."

"His debt shall be paid."

"Paid?"

"Not in full, but as much as is honestly due to him. I shall set a sensible solicitor to work to make a compromise."

"But the money? No, no; he will not give up. This is putting on the screw so as to move my sister."

"Whom he will not move," said Mark, smiling with content. "I suppose you are not likely to take up your father's invention?"

"Good gracious, no! Millington, our big swell, told me, when I mentioned it, that it was a craze, and that it was contrary to nature. You can't arrest ordinary decay."

"No, of course not; life must go on till it reaches its highest pitch, and then decline."

"Of course."

"Well, look here, Hendon; Janet and I have a little money between us in Consols, and, as we are going to make a fresh start together, we'll do so clearly, and your debt shall be paid."

"What, with Janet's money? Hang it, no!" cried Hendon fiercely; "I'm not such a cad as that."

"You are going to be my brother," said Mark, smiling as he clapped him on the shoulder, "my younger brother, and you'll do exactly what I bid you."

"Yes, but—"

"That will do. I see my way clearly now, so let's go up-stairs and have a chat with the girls."

Hendon put down his pipe very slowly, and glanced up at a shelf, upon which some of the apparatus connected with his father's dreams was standing; but it offered him no solution of his difficulties, and he followed Mark Heath into the surgery just as Janet and Rich, who were unable longer to bear the suspense, came down to press for an explanation.

"Here, I say," saluted the party, from Bob, "who's been a-meddlin' with these here prep'rations?"

"What preparations?" said Hendon sharply.

"These here," cried Bob, who had just taken down a large glass jar to dust. "The doctor will be in a way. He don't like no one to meddle with them."

The jar was labeled, like the row from which it had been taken, with a gummed-on slip of letter-paper, the contents being written in the doctor's own bold hand, the ink now yellow with age, and the gummed-on label beginning to peel off.

"Put the horrible thing away!" cried Hendon angrily.

"But some 'un's been a-stuffing something else in here as don't belong," cried the boy. "I knows 'em all by heart. Look here!"

He thrust his hand into the glass jar, after removing the great stopper.

"What are you doing, boy?" cried Hendon, stepping forward to arrest the lad's action, as he drew out, all dripping with the spirit, a disgusting-looking swollen object, evidently a portion of the digestive viscera of a calf or sheep; but before he could reach him, Mark uttered a wild cry, thrust him aside; and, as he snatched the hideous-looking object from Bob's hand, the glass jar fell upon the surgery floor, was smashed to atoms, and a strong odor of methylated spirit filled the place.

"You've done it now!" cried the boy piteously; and then he stared as Mark dragged from his pocket a knife, and cut the string of what, in place of an anatomical preparation, was a soaked and swollen washleather bag.

"Look, Rich, look!" cried Mark, dropping the knife, his hands trembling with excitement, and his voice so husky and changed that it was hardly recognizable.

As he spoke, he thrust Rich back upon the settee, and, with one quick motion, poured a couple of handfuls of rough diamonds into her lap.

"Mark!" she cried, as he sank upon his knees before her, and clasped her hands; while, in his excitement, Hendon caught Janet in his arms, from which she might have extricated herself a little more quickly than she did.

"Now just look at that!" said Bob, picking up the bag, which had fallen upon the floor. "Why, it's just like one o' them things as the doctor's got saved up. I say," he continued excitedly, "lookye here sir, there's another one inside."

He drew out of the swollen leather bag a stone as big as a small marble, and held it out.

"Yes; and that's yours, my boy," cried Mark excitedly; "whatever it fetches shall be for you."

"What! my own?" cried Bob.

"Yes—yes!"

"To do what I like with, sir?"

"Well, it shall be applied for your benefit, my lad."

"Then I wants some on it now!" cried the boy excitedly.

"What for?" said Rich.

"To get my old ooman home."

"And I want one, Mark," cried Hendon.

"Yes," said Mark; "to pay James Poynter's debt."

CHAPTER XVIII.

KNOTTING UP LOOSE THREADS.

It had been the doctor's last act before he admitted his assailants. As if inspired by a fear that his patient's excited utterances might be true, and urged by the risk of leaving so valuable a treasure unprotected, he had taken the bag, and slipped it in a place not likely to be examined, though he never recovered sufficiently to recall what he had done.

As to the two men who had visited the surgery that night, by a strange want of scent on the part of the sleuth-hounds of the law they were never found; one reason being that, with the cash they found in the belt Mark Heath wore, they had made their way back to the Cape.

The house in Ramillies Street remained unchanged

in aspect save that after a time, under the old doctor's name, a new plate was affixed, bearing that of his son.

The red light shone out every night, and the plates upon the door glistened in the sunshine, such little as came into the street, after Bob had been over the said plates with rotten-stone and oil, prior to "cleaning hisself," as he called it, and donning his new smart livery, ready to admit the patients who came; but though James Poynter was often really sick, he sought advice there no more.

That red light shone out every night with a dull glare across the road; but whenever as ordinary constable, or later on as sergeant, John Whyley's duties took him round that way, he always stopped, and rolled his head in his stock with a sapient shake.

"Ah!" he invariably said; "that there just was a fog!"

[THE END.]

www.ingramcontent.com/pod-product-compliance
Lightning Source LLC
Chambersburg PA
CBHW020302170426
43202CB00008B/467